ARIADNE'S AWAKENING

Taking up the threads of consciousness

by

Signe Schaefer

Betty Staley

Margli Matthews

HAWTHORN PRESS

Published by Hawthorn Press,
The Mount, Whiteshill, Stroud, Gloucestershire, United Kingdom.
ISBN 1 869890 01 9
Typeset in Plantin by Glevum Graphics, 2 Honyatt Road, Gloucester.
Printed by Billings & Sons Limited, Worcester.
Cover design by Helen Williams.

"Dutch Interior" appeared in the 1971 edition of
A Grain of Mustard Seed by May Sarton.
Reproduced by kind permission of W. W. Norton & Co., New York.

Contents

For Ariadne . . .
who helped us to pick up
the thread of consciousness.

Introduction

In June 1977, a group of women gathered together in Sacramento, California for a conference called *Women and the Challenge of Consciousness*. For the organizers this was a bold step. It was our first attempt at publicly addressing questions dear to our hearts. The conference was much more exciting than we had ever imagined and proved to be only the beginning of an on-going and ever-widening work.

For three years already we had been meeting together in various groupings – first in the small town of Forest Row in England and then later, for some, in California. What drew that first group together in the autumn of 1974 was the desire to better understand what being women, in this time in history, was all about. We were all interested in the spiritual perspectives of human development presented by Dr Rudolf Steiner, the Austrian philosopher, scientist and founder of Anthroposophy and of Waldorf Education; we wanted to connect these ideas to our questions as women.

Some of us had been directly involved in the women's movement in the late Sixties and early Seventies; others had watched and read and thought; but all of us felt that there was a missing dimension in the general debate. We could, of course, see the need for political and economic changes, but we felt there were even more basic things to struggle for. We wanted to know more about what it really means to live in a woman's – or a man's – body. And, what is it that lives in this body? We felt strongly that our 'I' is not essentially female or male, and yet clearly it makes an enormous difference in our development through a lifetime if this 'I' is experiencing life as a woman or as a man. These questions were both very personal and very general – we knew they reached right through our private relationships, and out to the whole of our modern society.

We felt that Rudolf Steiner, with his perspectives on the human being as a reincarnating being and with his extensive view of the evolution of consciousness, might offer us clues; and so we sought together to explore some of his ideas. But we also had a very strong dedication to basing our explorations on our own experiences. So we built our weekly meetings out of our shared, personal questions: about being individuals, wives, daughters, mothers, lovers, friends and co-workers. We shared the desire of so many women for consciousness raising, but we sought consciousness of our spiritual dimensions as well, and of our real responsibilities as women. We felt sure that the impulse behind the women's movement was about more than only better jobs, or better pay, or better sex.

The different groups meandered on their various ways, sometimes using books for focus (*The Way of All Women* by M. Esther Harding was particularly helpful), always talking, listening, exchanging experiences and insights. Finally a few of us decided to offer the workshop in California. At that point we had little experience in organizing workshops or in giving lectures. Our preparations were mixed with some trepidation! But the women who came to the conference put us at ease – they too felt the significance, even the urgency, of the questions. The material and explorations we shared were so much more important than our own individual nervousness.

When the conference was over, there was a question about printing up the lectures as study material. It seemed like a good idea . . . but good ideas are seldom simple! Two years, and many late nights later, there were several potential 'chapters' but no publisher. Over the years many thoughts wove back and forth between us, creating the fabric that would become this book.

In the meantime much else was developing. In Forest Row, the Ariadne Working Group was founded and began offering workshops, fostering the development of support groups, and publishing an international newsletter. More recently there have been similar working groups in Holland and the U.S.A. as well as many support groups around the world.

There are now many more books than in the early Seventies which acknowledge the spiritual dimensions of questions raised by the women's movement. Attitudes have changed considerably and there is much more valuing within individual women and men of their own feminine and masculine sides. The 'feminine' as such is not so undervalued and balance is more sought after – at least in our words. Yet I fear sometimes that we rush too fast, thinking we have really changed because our words are changing. The feminine dimension – in an individual or in our culture – needs time and space in which to grow strong enough to be a truly balancing force. Lip-service is not enough. If, for example, parents say, "yes, we really should spend more quality time with the children" but continue full-steam toward their personal goals, the enhanced awareness becomes an empty shell. If more women join the work force but the ways of working remain unchanged, then there has been no real improvement.

In the last twenty years women have grown as a political and economic force. More women can fulfill a much broader range of personal goals. But there is also much loneliness, much isolation and confusion as roles change and expectations meet reality. Now is not an easy time for women and men who seek to be conscious of themselves and responsible to their tasks. But it is an exciting time and an important time. It is toward our common challenge for greater consciousness and balance that we offer this book.

There are so many people to thank when we review how this material came into being. All of the women – and many men too – who have participated in groups and workshops over the years have enhanced our insights and our lives. Our colleagues in the different Ariadne working groups are as much part of this book as we are and our gratitude and love for them is ongoing.

Judy and Martin Large are much more than valued publishers; that this book has finally come to be printed is due to their persistence, encouragement and ongoing friendship.

To our husbands and our children, we give our very special thanks: for helping us keep real our many discoveries of what being women is all about.

Signe Eklund Schaefer
June 1985

Dutch Interior
Pieter de Hooch (1629-1682)

I recognize the quiet and the charm,
This safe enclosed room where a woman sews
And life is tempered, orderly, and calm.

Through the Dutch door, half open, sunlight streams
And throws a pale square down on the red tiles.
The cosy black dog suns himself and dreams.

Even the bed is sheltered, it encloses,
A cupboard to keep people safe from harm,
Where copper glows with the warm flush of roses.

The atmosphere is all domestic, human,
Chaos subdued by the sheer power of need.
This is a room where I have lived as woman,

Lived too what the Dutch painter does not tell —
The wild skies overhead, dissolving, breaking,
And how that broken light is never still,

And how the roar of waves is always near,
What bitter tumult, treacherous and cold,
Attacks the solemn charm year after year!

It must be felt as peace won and maintained
Against those terrible antagonists —
How many from this quiet room have drowned?

How many left to go, drunk on the wind,
And take their ships into heartbreaking seas;
How many whom no woman's peace could bind?

Bent to her sewing, she looks drenched in calm.
Raw grief is disciplined to the fine thread.
But in her heart this woman is the storm;

Alive, deep in herself, holds wind and rain,
Remaking chaos into an intimate order
Where sometimes light flows through a windowpane.

May Sarton

Feminine and Masculine
through balance toward freedom

Signe Eklund Schaefer

The Problem

In my twenties, as a wife and mother of two small children, one of the central themes of my life moved into clear focus. It took the form of a question which reverberated ever more loudly into all aspects of my daily life: 'Why am I a woman now?' I became aware that I must have once lived quite securely in my sense of being a person; but now my being a woman took on special significance, made new demands, presented new challenges. From the beginning the question had two interweaving aspects: Why am 'I' experiencing this life as a woman – what do I meet, learn, give and develop as a woman that I would be unable to do as a man? And, why now, at this point in history, this crucial time of 'women's liberation'? As I faced the totality of the question, I felt a growing need to become more self-aware, more inwardly reflective, and at the same time my social responsibility was aroused.

In my early contact with the Women's Movement I was struck by how easily our thoughts stayed with the polarity of woman-man. But for me, this was not an adequate place to rest my questions. As much as I knew I was a woman, I knew that I was more than this too. So it seemed necessary to look also at the polarity of feminine and masculine qualities – to view them not only as the exclusive attributes of women or men respectively, but as forces, archetypal principles existing in both women and men.

And of course these qualities are not only evident in individuals. Their continuous interplay is basic to all relationships as well. The interaction may be quite subtle and multileveled – certainly it is not limited to the external picture of a relationship between a woman and a man. In fact, the coming together and struggle for balance of feminine and masculine qualities penetrates the whole of our culture, is a main, underlying current in our human social development.

At all levels – within the individual, in relationships, and in the whole of society – it becomes increasingly urgent that we recognize the difference between the polarity of woman-man and that of feminine-masculine. Many women blame men for all the ills of modern life, for the social chaos which surrounds us. Without denying that men have of course played a part in creating the difficulties of today, it seems that the problem is much more the over-dominance of masculine influence in us all. It is not just a problem of men, but of our whole modern, materialistic way of thinking and being. The essentially positive masculine qualities – for example, individualization, analysis, and objectivity – have in a sense gone overboard, become extreme and decadent; and so we are surrounded by selfishness, exploitation, and anonymity. Employers value the 'aggressive self-starter', even more if he or she is single and thus unencumbered. We are surrounded by images of 'me first' and 'each-man-for-himself'. We are treated, and can come to treat others as faceless numbers. Even our bodies are likened to a machine, with replaceable parts. Individuals feel increasingly cut off from each other and severed from any divine order.

It seems to me important to try to understand why and how humanity has come to this point and also to consider where we are going. If we recognize a situation which is out of balance – in our own individuality, in any relationship, or in social life generally – can we do anything to readjust the scales, to bring about a more fruitful interaction? Must the forces of feminine and masculine merely surge through us or can we learn to use these different qualities with growing consciouness and responsibility?

During the last twenty years the Women's Movement has raised many vital questions and focused attention on areas of damaging inequity. The early emphasis on consciousness raising brought new depth to many people's lives, and the political action born out of the movement has created new opportunities for women in a wide range of fields. There is of course still much to be done in terms of broadening job possibilities and easing rigidified role definitions. Can we remember though that we are confronting several levels of imbalance? It is all too easy to get stuck at the physical, material level of the 'women's question' – and so then to blame only 'men'. The material level is important, but it is not the only one. The soul and the spirit of human beings require a movement toward 'liberation' at least as much as the body does.

I see a strong and tragically modern example of the need to be aware of these different levels in the issue of rape. As a bodily assault its damage is all too apparent; we recognize as well that a physical rape leaves psychological and emotional scars on the assaulted woman. We even speak quite rightly about the rape of our physical earth, our natural resources. But how aware are we of the more invisible rape that goes on every day in the soul and spirit dimensions of all modern people – through the excessive technology which surrounds us, through the confrontation tactics of our interactions, through the anonymity and isolation of our modern life? However are we to recognize and understand these assaults? And what can we do to prevent them and to make possible other forms of interaction than those of force or consumption or facelessness?

Surely the increase in physical violence so disturbing in our times can be seen as an outward manifestation of the inner disorder and despair of modern human beings. We must of course find practical ways to deal with these outer troubles; but equally we must search to discover the deeper causes which underlie so much social unrest. All of which brings me back to the question of feminine and masculine. Not only women, but the feminine in us all has been attacked and oppressed – and is now struggling to find new value for itself, is trying to awaken to new responsibilities, is attempting to fulfill newly emerging needs for the further development of humanity.

If I question my being a woman 'now', I necessarily imply the significance of a change through time: Now is the present, but the present in relation to the past and to the future. It seems crucial to me that we try to understand our modern situation – with all its virtues and all its severe difficulties – from the perspective of a development through time. We must not lean back nostalgically on bygone days, nor miss today in anticipation of what might be coming someday; but a true attention to the present moment, and an awake responsibility to its needs, can be enormously enhanced by a developmental perspective. How else are we to avoid getting stuck in the mire of today? Of course we all do get stuck – at many levels: In a despairing moment of self-analysis, in a knotty patch within a relationship, in a raging frustration at some impossibility of modern life. As long as we go round and round the particular spot we are stuck in, there is no movement – and no real solution. It is only when we step away for a moment, take a longer view or broader perspective, that suddenly we can breathe again and move on. So if I say that the feminine – in women and in men and in our modern society – has been attacked and oppressed and is now seeking new ways of being and new value, then I want to understand why. Was oppression necessary? Were there ever times of greater balance of these archetypal forces? Or a time even before division? Could there ever be a true lasting unity? What really is this fundamental polarity in the human experience all about?

It was in working with a group of other women that these questions became more and more important to me. We all shared an interest in considering these questions from a personal, a historical and a spiritual perspective. Even stating it that way is not adequate, for the personal is also spiritual, the spiritual also historical – the dimensions interweave, the levels are interdependent. It has already been stated that the work of Rudolf Steiner was a fundamental source of both insight and ever new questions in our efforts to understand the levels of interaction between feminine and masculine forces. Other chapters of this book deal with the relationship of feminine and masculine qualities in each individual and within relationships.

For this chapter I want to draw on that aspect of Rudolf Steiner's work which gives a picture of cosmic evolution, of the development through vast time of the earth and of human beings and of our particular place in the whole cosmos. Here Steiner is describing not the individual journey of a single human ego through time, but the collective development, and even mission, of humanity as a whole. From his perspective of human beings as reincarnating individualities he suggests that we have all partaken in this cosmic evolution; in fact through the passage of time we have emerged more and more as separated individualities, particular beings who have become through our separation – not only from each other but from the determination of the divine world as well – ever more responsible for the continuing evolution of the cosmos.

But how are we to understand this human responsibility, to see the meaning of our place within the whole cosmic evolution? Sometimes I question if it is possible to imagine anything so grand. But then I feel we must – not out of arrogance and self-centred presumption but with wonder for the whole creative process and with humility in the face of our human tasks. Rudolf Steiner spoke out of his direct spiritual perceptions about realities which existed long before anything we can support by geological or archeological evidence. I have no such direct experience to relate; but I am moved by his descriptions and I feel an essential truth in the progression he presents.

Origins

Steiner describes vast realms of being, gives a picture of a very gradual process of condensation and materialization of the earth and of human beings up to our present time. He looks into the distant past, and also towards a far future time. Because a central concern of this chapter is the interweaving of feminine and masculine within the human experience, I use as the starting point in my developmental picture what he refers to as the "division of the sexes". This transpired (and again I must emphasize, it took place over a very long period of time) during what he refers to as the Lemurian stage of the evolution of the earth. He describes Lemuria as a continent which existed well over one million years ago, south of what is now Asia, roughly in the area between Madagascar and Sri Lanka. Human beings were gradually materializing out of a previously non-physical state of being, but in no way yet into any form we would today recognize as 'human' bodies. [1]

Initially these human beings were not differentiated into female and male; but they had the potential forces of both feminine and masculine within them. In Steiner's words: "For only in the course of time did the forms of man and woman develop from an older, basic form in which human beings were neither one nor the other, but rather were both at once. He who wants to form an idea of these enormously distant periods of the past must however liberate himself completely from what man sees around him. . . At that time the human body still consisted of soft and malleable materials. The other forms of earth were also still soft and malleable. As opposed to its later and hardened condition, earth was still in a welling, more fluid one." [2]

Furthermore, these beings reproduced themselves through a kind of divinely ordered self-impregnation. They existed in a pre-conscious state of unity with the spiritual world, without birth and death as we know it. Rather than actual birth, propagation "was like an out-pressure from human beings who were ripe to continue their own development." [3] Steiner also indicates a time in the far future when human beings will again be uni-sexual, androgynous beings but now with a self-acquired ability to reproduce themselves through the power of the Word: "And this in the future will be the birth of the new human being – that he is spoken forth by another." [4] From a time of unconscious unity, the human being divided into female and male. This division into women and men, with feminine and masculine forces within them, has lasted for long epochs and will continue for a long time yet; but gradually will come a time of re-unity, now out of the conscious activity of evolving human beings.

This all makes a remarkable picture – hard to grasp firmly, but possible perhaps to just hold, carefully, tenderly. Steiner goes on to illuminate this picture of the division of the sexes by linking it to the evolution of the capacity for human thinking and thus for the possibility of developing an individual, self-conscious relationship to the spirit:

"Thus man could use a portion of the energy which previously he employed for the production of beings like himself, in order to perfect his own nature. The force by which mankind forms a thinking brain for itself is the same by which man impregnated himself in ancient times. The price of thought is single-sexedness. By no longer impregnating themselves, but rather by impregnating each other, human beings can turn a part of their productive energy within, and so become thinking creatures. Thus the male and female body each represent an imperfect external embodiment of the soul, but thereby they become more perfect creatures inwardly."[5]

The energy previously used for self-impregnation went inward and fostered the creation of a new physical organ – the brain – which could then become the vehicle for the entry of the eternal spirit. This division of the sexes and consequent redirection of energy which allowed human beings to become thinking beings, happened long ago and yet it repeats itself over again as children go through puberty. Just when the young person's body declares its sexual maturity – crossing over into womanhood or manhood – there is also a dawning of a new capacity for thinking, and a whole new self-consciousness and movement toward independence.

There are so many remembrances of this fundamental link between sexual differentiation and thinking – thinking now not as dry abstracting, but as a creative act which connects us to, and makes us responsible within, the whole of evolution. The recollection is clear with the word 'conceive'. We conceive a child through the union of woman and man. We conceive a thought when we bring together what Rudolf Steiner refers to in connection with the division into sexes as "the seed-force of the soul and spirit" and a "life-giving, quickening force."[6]

The phrase "conception of life" always reverberates within me through layers of significance. How we conceive life (i.e. a baby), and how we conceive of life itself are questions which demand our attention as modern people. They are totally inter-related questions: How we view either one – as a mainly physical question or including a spiritual dimension – has effect on the other. If we will recognize the questions, they challenge us profoundly, ask us to grow in both consciousness and responsibility.

The ancient command "know thyself" holds echoes of the polarity of feminine and masculine as well as a challenge towards inner balance. In the Bible Adam 'knew' Eve and the Patriarchs 'knew' their wives; and they conceived. This knowing signified both sexual union and spiritual fructification. Much of our modern knowledge – about the world or about ourselves – seems dry, abstract, lifeless; yet the challenge lies within us to make it dynamic, creative, to bring it ever again to a new birth within us.

In the picture of paradise before the Fall, I see an image of that time before the division of the sexes. God created the original man "male and female" in his own image. Until they ate of the fruit of the Tree of Knowledge, Adam and Eve were androgynous, undifferentiated, "not ashamed". When Eve desired the tree "to make one wise" she took a step toward independent consciousness, toward becoming "as gods, knowing good and evil". This was an enormous step – out of a divinely ordained, dream-like existence toward individual freedom. But the price of this freedom was the God-given power of self-procreation. When Eve ate the fruit she became 'woman' and in giving it to Adam, she gave away her ability to be self-impregnating. Now she must be physically fertilized by 'man'. And he must go forth out of Paradise into the world of material, sense-based reality, and work and till the soil.

This new 'fallen' man has to meet the world in an entirely new way and so develop, through what Rudolf Steiner calls "masculine striving", a new kind of knowledge about the world. By collecting and combining impressions from his environment he can bring forth a new physical creative strength. Steiner contrasts this masculine striving to what he refers to as an older female wisdom, a "received Godly strength". The female wisdom Steiner suggests was carried historically as "priestly wisdom" – it reflected an intuitive union with the spiritual world and was embodied through many varied religious images and practices.[7] Here is an echo of another polarity of the soul which was originally connected to the division of the sexes. In *Cosmic Memory* Steiner says: "The male body has taken a form which is conditioned by the element of will; the female body on the other hand bears the stamp of imagination."[8]

Even as a young girl I wondered why it was Eve who first ate the forbidden fruit. I could never accept the explanation about the sin of woman – it had to be more significant, and it did not seem essentially 'wrong'. As I grew older I found repeated pictures in mythology of an original wholeness, a primeval godly wisdom expressed in feminine images: A womb, an egg, a cow, the Waters, the Night, the Great Round, the Mother of all Things.

My readings in anthroposophy and feminine research confirmed the picture of an older female-like existence and influence: "The female sex was the first. The female power was the earlier . . .";[9] but the male power brought about physical man. With a coming of a masculine force – a force for materialization, individualization and differentiation – humanity began its descent from the divine world, came out of paradise and into reality, into female and male bodies through which human beings could now experience birth and death, good and evil, and the possibility of developing an individual consciousness and freedom.

So Eve, as a female figure, is to me an echo of that earlier female influence. But the development of humanity necessitated the entrance of the masculine force, and in order to gain influence for itself this masculine striving needed to do battle with the all-encompassing feminine dominance. By the time the Old Testament was written down, the masculine was coming into control, but the shadows of the old still lingered; and so Eve had to be made the 'sinner', the temptress. The feminine, unconscious union with the divine – embodied in woman – had to be subjugated if the emerging sense of individuality was to be encouraged.

Rudolf Steiner, feminist researchers, and much of mythology all suggest an actual battle taking place between feminine and masculine. The question is what is the battle for, and who is really fighting it? That it is a war for power between women and men seems such a limited, and even tragic, view; for what would constitute victory? Steiner sees this struggle between feminine and masculine as an essential aspect in the development of human consciousness.[10] The aim is not in endless separation, but in finally bringing these forces into a dynamic and creative harmony within each individual, and through the free and loving coming together of individuals, within all of humanity.

A conscious, creative harmony of opposites cannot just happen; it must be developed over time. The different elements must have their periods of active growth and periods of rest, phases of dominance and of recession. I have suggested that this has been the case with the feminine and masculine principles. I would like now to trace further some of the steps of this progression because doing so can spread new light on the struggles of our modern age and give us a sense of direction as we look toward the future.

The Great Mother

Most early mythologies speak of a time before division, a time of self-contained wholeness, of unified primeval wisdom, of chaos before creation. Existence is as in a womb, in an essential receptivity, in darkness and in water. Often, out of this mythic chaos of possibility emerges a Great Mother figure: Tiamat in the ancient Babylonian creation myth *Enumah Elish* was initially chaos, flux, the primeval salt-water and "she who bore them all;"[11] Eurynome, the Goddess of All Things in the Pelasgian creation story, "rose naked from chaos" to dance lonely upon the waters;[12] and in the Olympian creation myth, "At the beginning of all things Mother Earth emerged from Chaos and bore her son Uranus as she slept."[13]

The influence, the domain, the dominance of the Great Goddess was absolute. Helen Diner says of Ishtar, the Great Mother of Babylon: "She was the uterus at rest, which was the earth, around which the entire cosmos rotated. Her belt was the zodiac, she was the morning and the evening star, the creatress of all things, the great huntress, the mistress of battle, the queen of heaven and earth, the horned moon goddess, mother of gods and men, . . ."[14] The representations of the great goddess are many: Ishtar in Babylonia, Isis in Egypt, Demeter in Greece – Mother Nature in a variety of faces and aspects. But always she has to do with nurturing, with the Earth and the Moon, with birth and death. She watches over agriculture, tends the hearth, and encourages humanity towards civilization.

The Great Goddess was revered because the influence of the Mother was absolute. The Mother was by necessity first – her son might be prophesied, his day would come, but for long ages she reigned as the original, all-nourishing power. As Robert Graves states: "Ancient Europe had no gods. The Great Goddess was regarded as immortal, changeless, and omnipotent; and the concept of fatherhood had not been introduced into religious thought. She took lovers, but for pleasure, not to provide her children with a father. Men feared, adored, and obeyed the matriarch; the hearth which she tended in a cave or hut being their earliest social centre, and motherhood their prime mystery."[15]

When Rudolf Steiner speaks of the early women of Lemuria and later Atlantis (a stage of evolution between the Lemurian and the present condition of humanity and the earth), he gives a fascinating picture of feminine influence. In keeping with the differentiation of forces embodied in the division of the sexes, he speaks of how girls of Lemuria were trained to develop a strong imagination: "For example she was exposed to the storm in order to calmly feel its dreadful beauty; she had to witness the combat of the men fearlessly, filled only with a feeling of appreciation for the strength and power she saw before her. Thereby propensities for dreaming and for fantasy developed in the girl, and these were highly valued."[16] The boys, on the other hand, were educated to develop the faculty of will: "The boys were hardened in the strongest manner. They had to learn to undergo dangers, to overcome pain, to accomplish daring deeds."[17]

Due to the special powers which the early women developed they had great influence and leadership over evolving humanity. I quote Rudolf Steiner at length here because the vision into this past time is his:

"The development of mankind can only be correctly understood by the one who takes into consideration that the first progress in the life of the imagination was made by woman. The development connected with the imagination, with the formation of memory, of customs which formed the seeds for a life of law, for a kind of morals, came from this side. If man had seen and exercised the forces of nature, woman became the first *interpreter* of them."[18] (his italics) ". . . Through her memory, woman had acquired the capacity to make the experiences and adventures of the past useful for the future. What had proved helpful yesterday she used today and realized that it would also be useful tomorrow. The institutions for a communal life therefore emanated from her. Under her influence the concepts of 'good and evil' developed. Through her thoughtful life she acquired an understanding for nature. Out of the observation of nature, those ideas developed in her according to which she directed the actions of men. The leaders had arranged things in such a way that through the soul of woman, the wilful nature, the vigorous strength of man were ennobled and refined. Of course one must represent all this to oneself as childish beginnings. The words of our language all too easily call up ideas which are taken from the life of the present."[19]

A good reminder that. How really can we look back so far – with our present consciousness, our present language – and not feel lost, or disbelieving? Perhaps it is all a grand myth, and perhaps even the myths can tell us nothing 'real' of times past. But I feel deep within me that they can. As remembrance of humanity's connection to the spiritual world, mythology seems to me a valuable source for prehistorical images of the development of consciousness. Rudolf Steiner speaks of how the early mythologies look back into 'the workshop of creation'.[20] I find that a very powerful image. The myths hold echoes of a once living reality; at the same time they show us something of the state of consciousness of the people who heard these echoes – in so many diverse ways.

It is important not to look for rigid chronologies within the myths but to see where patterns emerge in the different stories. Since stages of consciousness do not always peacefully replace one another, the battle and overthrows in legends can be seen as expressing the shifts, the gradual changes in an entire view of nature and of the cosmos. The remarkable thing is that the most diverse myths do show similar patterns, basic themes and struggles.

The worship of the Great Goddess into historical times surely reflected and inspired the kind of feminine influence and responsibility which Steiner characterized as part of Lemurian and Atlantean civilizations. And yet with few exceptions, archeologists and cultural historians have until recently ignored data which suggested an early predominance of women or which supported a widespread matriarchal culture. One 19th century exception was Johann Jacob Bachofen who developed a theory of cultural evolution based on a picture of an inner, spiritual development of humanity. His study of myth and early social custom suggested no isolated aberrations of feminine influence, but rather that: "All these traits join to form a single picture and lead to the conclusion that mother right is not confined to any particular people but marks a cultural stage. In view of the universal qualities of human nature, this cultural stage cannot be restricted to any particular ethnic family. And consequently what must concern us is not so much the similarities between isolated phenomena as the unity of the basic conception . . . 1) mother right belongs to a cultural period preceding that of the patriarchal system; 2) it began to decline only with the victorious development of the paternal system."[21]

More modern researchers, among them many Feminists, have recognized the significance of recent archeological finds in present-day Turkey. The discoveries by James Mellaart at Catal Huyuk (a city which now appears to date back over 9,000 years)[22] give a clear picture of matriarchal society and validate many of Bachofen's ideas. The wall paintings, the clay figurines, the burial practices and even the architecture of this ancient ceremonial centre suggest the worship of the Great Mother and a peaceful, agricultural existence where women were influential and revered. Likewise in the development of Greek civilization the matriarchal significance of Minoan and Mycenaean cultures is now widely recognized. Wherever archeologists study the early times of Goddess worship, they find evidence of the civilizing influence of women: of their roles in the development of agriculture, linked as it was to lunar rhythms; of their tasks as potters, weavers, spinners; of their significance in the beginnings of language and ritual and religious practice; of their functions as queens, priestesses, seers and healers.[23]

Men and women existed for a long time before the principle of duality entered even dimly into human consciousness.[24] An expression of this gradual dawning of an awareness of division is evident in the mythological theme of the Great Mother and her Son. Out of the oneness – the wholeness – is born a new element, that force of physical creative strength, of masculine striving. Tiamat becomes ever more dark and demoniacal, the enveloping force of the night which must yield to the dawn of light. In time, Marduk rises up against her now destructive, devouring power and divides her body into Heaven and Earth. Likewise he assigns the gods to one realm or the other: "Though alike revered, into two they shall be divided."[25]

This theme of the Great Mother and the struggle of her Son to overcome her is an archetypal picture of a stage in the feminine – masculine struggle, and it takes innumerable forms. The old, unconscious feminine union of all cannot go on ruling. Its all-encompassing nature becomes smothering, devouring, and allows no space for the individual or for the development of freedom.

But the Mother Goddess does not always become wicked; sometimes she develops as the good mother, bestowing care and affection, preparing for and ultimately yielding to the ascendence of her son. Erich Neumann in *The Origins and History of Consciousness* speaks of a growing ambivalence toward the Great Mother experienced by the waking ego of humanity: "The devouring, destructive aspect . . . is seen figuratively as the evil mother, whether as the bloodstained goddess of death, plague, famine, flood, and the force of instinct, or as the sweetness that lures to destruction. But, as the good mother, she is fullness and abundance; the dispenser of life and happiness, the nutrient earth, the cornucopia of the fruitful

womb. She is mankind's instinctive experience of the world's depth
and beauty, of the goodness and graciousness of Mother Nature who
daily fulfills the promise of redemption and resurrection, of new life
and birth."[26]

In the figure of the Egyptian Great Goddess Isis we can find a
significant shift in the relationship of feminine and masculine
influence. Isis and Osiris – sister and brother, wife and husband –
were great beings. To us, their story can seem long and complicated,
developing contradictions as its telling changes over time; but to the
ancient Egyptians it embodied a long series of facts related to the
evolution of the earth and of the whole solar system.[27] Isis was an
all-powerful goddess, she could find and restore Osiris to life after he
was killed and dismembered by their wicked brother Set; but with the
birth of her son Horus, she makes an essential transition to the 'Good
Mother'. In this regard, Steiner says of her: "A deep mystery, heavily
veiled, manifests itself in the figure of Isis, the lovable goddess who, in
the spiritual consciousness of the ancient Egyptian, was present with
the Horus child as our Madonna is present today with the Jesus child.
. . We must see deep mysteries in Isis, mysteries that are grounded in
the spiritual. The Madonna is a remembrance of Isis: Isis appears
again in the Madonna."[28]

The son Horus is conceived after Osiris' death, but Isis struggles
with the gods to have them accept Osiris as his father. As Neumann
says: "It is an essential function of the 'good' Isis to give up her
matriarchal dominance, which was such an obvious feature in the
original matriarchate of Egyptian Queens. Typical of this surrender,
and of the transition to the patriarchal system, is Isis' struggle to get
the legitimacy of her son Horus recognized by the gods. Whereas in . .
. (a matriarchal system) a son is always the son of his mother, Isis
fights for the recognition of the paternity of Osiris for Horus, who is to
take over from him the paternal inheritance of the patriarchate. On
this inheritance was based the lineage of the Egyptian Pharoahs, each
of whom styled himself 'Son of Horus'."[29]

In ancient Egypt, mythology and history begin to come together to
tell the same story. The old matriarchal consciousness, as a universal
cultural stage, was on its way out and patriarchal importance would
grow ever stronger. The brother – sister marriages were a reflection of
this shift. Inheritance initially passed through the woman but if a man
wanted to maintain a family wealth or power for himself or for his
children, he could marry his sister. Gradually this pattern led to a

form of patriarchal inheritance. "Throughout Egyptian social history there was a tendency to abolish the matriarchal order. It began with a decline in magical functions. During the first several dynasties, there often were female names listed amoung the lists of priests; they disappeared after the twelfth dynasty (that is, after 1785 B.C.) with the exception of the royal princesses who held sacerdotal offices by virtue of their birth."[30]

Always with the question of feminine and masculine there is this interweaving of levels: Women carry the line of succession in a matriarchal time; the revered goddess bows to her husband and there are gradually fewer women priests; a decline in 'magical functions' heralds the coming of a masculine influence. Rudolf Steiner gives a picture of humanity gradually emerging from the 'womb of divinity',[31] from the union with and unconscious clairvoyant experience of the spiritual world. In terms of his cosmology, I have made an enormous leap from Lemuria to ancient Egypt, hurled over vast ages and ignored highly developed civilizations. I recommend anyone with an interest in these questions to read Steiner's descriptions of what he calls the post-Atlantean epochs.[32] I have begun with the third of these, the Egypto-Chaldean epoch – and thus skipped over his descriptions of ancient Indian and Persian civilizations – because with this third phase we begin to have historical records which can validate something of the progression of consciousness along the feminine-masculine pole. Here we can find evidence of humanity's movement out of a direct connection to the spiritual world, out of a kind of maternal wholeness and union with the gods, into the beginnings of the conquest of physical reality by human faculties.

In ancient Egypt there was only a slow beginning of a sense-based experience of reality. The early Pharoahs were guided by divine inspiration; not until after 2200 B.C. with the end of the Old Kingdom, did this direct inspiration gradually diminish. Even then through their mystery teachings and mythology the Egyptians could acquire an intuitive perception of the relationship between the human being and the cosmos, and so they could build the pyramids with remarkable astronomical precision.

Though building their cultures in the same basic period, Steiner says that the early Sumerian, Chaldean and Babylonian peoples were more strongly inclined to the physical, sensible world than were the Egyptians.[33] They investigated cosmic phenomena to determine earthly laws. They invented writing – translating living thought into symbols – and they created units of measurement reflecting the relationship of microcosm to macrocosm, of man to the starry heavens. They also told the story of Gilgamesh, the part god, part human king who proclaimed: 'I am Gilgamesh, and it must be that I shall see everything, learn everything, understand everything.'[34] It was he who defied the Goddess Ishtar, and he who mourned the death of his beloved friend Enkidu and so experienced the problem of immortality.

Perception into the spiritual world was gradually dimming as human consciousness focused ever more on sense-based reality. Both interest in and dependence on the physical realm were growing stronger. The Egyptians mummified the dead that the body should not perish; they sought to retain and glorify this outer physical form of human experience.

This period that I have been describing coincides with the entrance into what the Indians call Kali Yuga – the Dark Age – in about 3100 B.C., an age which lasted until the end of the last century. 'It was dark because direct perception of the spiritual world became by its end almost wholly extinct.'[35] For the Egyptians and Chaldeans this direct spiritual perception was only beginning to yield to the possibilities of sense-based knowing:

"As man learned to elicit from the physical world of sense the laws of the Spiritual that underlie it, the sciences came into being; and as he came to recognize and manipulate the forces of this world, arts and crafts arose; man began to have his tools and his technique. To a man of the Chaldean and Babylonian peoples the world of the senses was no longer an illusion. In its various kingdoms, in mountain and ocean, in wind and water, it was a revelation of the spiritual deeds of Powers that were there behind it, whose laws he was studying to apprehend. To the Egyptian, the Earth was a field for his labour, given to him in a condition which it was his task so to transform by his own faculties of intelligence, that it might bear the stamp of man's ascendancy."[36]

Since those ancient times the human faculties of intelligence have wrought remarkable transformations. But today, far from reflecting a direct spiritual perception, much of our modern knowledge would deny even the possibility of existence of a spiritual world. And still, we have come out of the Dark Age. Kali Yuga ended in 1899 and in our

20th century more and more men and women express interest in exploring spiritual realms. And there has been a women's movement – and an ever stronger protest against the excessively rational, materialistic, technological and over-masculine nature of modern life.

But I jump ahead too fast – because I see a kind of fore-shadowing in Egypt of our present society, and reflections now of what began then.[37] I find it significant that with the beginning of Kali Yuga, the masculine influence begins to be felt; that by the end of this long Dark Age, what was so essential for the human development – the separation of the human individuality from the all-encompassing power of the gods – begins to imprison us and weld us forever to the physical plane.

But before really entering our present age, I want to return to the developing mythological-historical picture. And so I move to the world of ancient Greece, where the battle lines are more clearly drawn and the old matriarchal influence must finally succumb to the growing masculine force. Greek mythology gives many pictures of the struggle; certainly one of the most dramatic is the final defeat of the Amazons.

The Amazons can be seen as an image of the extreme end of the matriarchy – the desperate last stance of an over-ripe feminine stage of consciousness. These fierce women warriors worshipped the Goddess Artemis and lived in strict matriarchal tribes. Aggressively independent, they resisted marriage and mated only for procreation. Daughters were raised as full members of the tribe, while sons were sent back to the fathers' tribes or in some extreme cases maimed or killed.

The Amazons fought valiantly to the end; but after many celebrated battles, they, and the values and traditions they clung to, were defeated by the growing power of the Greek heroes: "The victories over the Amazons secured by Heracles, Theseus, Dionysus, Mopsus, and others, record, in fact, setbacks to the matriarchal system in Greece, Asia Minor, Thrace and Syria."[38]

Although they were completely overcome, the Amazons nevertheless remained as central figures in the folk imagination of the Greeks. They were remembered in art and festival, and revered long after their defeat, as if the Greeks recognized that some essential quality of human nature must go now inward to await further transformation. Though they were vanquished from the realm of earthly power, some essential quality they had represented would endure in their stories. Helen Diner speaks of this in her book *Mothers and Amazons:*

"To the Greco-Pelasgian world, they had seemed miraculous, surpassing mortal measure, more dangerous than all other nations put together and also more exacting... The wars between Greeks and Persians were wars between two male-dominated societies. In the Amazon war, the issue was which of the two forms of life was to shape European civilization in its image. The cleavage into sons and daughters had been unsettling even for the male victor, who sensed the polarity of human nature for the first time and with it the riddle of ultimate values."[39]

Many would question whether the Amazons were 'real'. I find the combined evidence strong enough to convince me that there were such tribes of war-like women; but even if there were not, their place in the imagination and developing consciousness of the Greeks cannot be denied. They forced into the extreme a way of life which humanity was in the process of outgrowing. Their ways rigidified and even caricatured the matriarchal stage of consciousness which once had been appropriate but which was being challenged to adapt to new developmental possibilities – just as today we are being challenged by an awakening feminine force, and some of our masculine ways, both in individuals and in our social forms, seem to rigidify in defensive reaction.

Pre-Hellenic Greece offers other, more clearly historical remnants of an ancient goddess-worshipping, matriarchal way of life as well, notably in the highly civilized cultures of Mycenae and Crete, which appear to have existed as far back as 4000 B.C. Artifacts from Mycenae and Cnossus reveal the all-pervasive influence of the Moon Goddess, as well as suggesting the many roles fulfilled by the women living there. However, from about 1500 B.C., patriarchal Indo-European tribes from the north began invading mainland Greece, until eventually they controlled the whole of the Peloponnese and succeeded in establishing a new religion under the leadership of their male god Zeus. This gradual invasion completed what many Feminists refer to as the 'Patriarchal Takeover'. To interpret this takeover as essentially about men oppressing women, and so limiting their possibilities, seems to me to ignore whole dimensions of a vital development in human consciousness. In her book *Androgyny: Toward a New Theory of Sexuality,* June Singer looks at the multileveled meaning of this fundamental shift:

"The Mother, first as the divine Earth herself, then in her many forms as Great Goddess, Mother Goddess, and also in her ruling role as human representative or queen ruling by authority of the Goddess, had held the human race in thralldom until the dawn of historical time. So it was, according to ancient traditions of many lands. Then in one place and then in another, men outgrew the childhood of the race and developed into rebellious adolescents, determined to assert their own wills and to exercise their capacity for active aggression. On the trans-personal level, father gods wrested power from the Great Mother Goddess and her company; and politically, the new patriarchies displaced the matriarchies of old."[40]

Separation

This idea of humanity being at a stage of rebellious adolescence, eager to assert its own will and come out of the mother's domain, is supported by many different aspects of classical Greek civilization. In the mythology with its tales of the heroes, in the birth of philosophy and science following the decline of the ancient mysteries, in city planning and the beginning of democracy, in the works of art modelled so beautifully on the human form – always there is an element of transition from old, divinely inspired, cosmic wisdom to a new kind of humanly acquired knowledge and power. Now the 'masculine striving' really begins to assert itself and to value individual skill and rationality as distinct from intuition, experience as distinct from faith, logical thought as distinct from clairvoyant awareness.

The individual human being was struggling to be born, to break free from the dominance of spiritual beings; and so we find many tales of human heroes, stories of human cleverness battling the no longer appropriate, and therefore destructive forces of an earlier clairvoyant sense of unity with the spiritual world. These forces, reflecting the fading maternal cosmic influence, were portrayed in the many monsters to be overcome by the heroes: the Sphinx, the Medusa, the Sirens, the Minotaur.

In the story from which the Ariadne Working Group took its name, Theseus, son of the King of Athens, goes to Crete to be sacrificed to the Minotaur. This beast, half human – half bull, was born out of Queen Pasiphae's passion for a white bull and was kept alive by her husband King Minos because of the lingering matriarchal power. Theseus and his Athenian companions were to be put into the Labyrinth, from which escape was impossible. Ariadne, the daughter of Queen Pasiphae and King Minos, falls in love with Theseus and determines to help him by giving him a ball of golden thread – that higher feminine life-sustaining force – with which he can find his way out of the Labyrinth again after slaying the beast. In gratitude for her help, Theseus marries Ariadne and they sail away; but he soon deserts her, asleep on the island of Naxos. Robert Graves says, "Why he did so must remain a mystery";[41] but it seems to me that in terms of feminine and masculine as influencing forces in the evolution of consciousness he had to leave her. Theseus can be seen as personifying the growing masculine force and it was time for this to develop, to pursue adventures and heroic exploits and so to move humanity forward toward individual responsibility and freedom from the dictates of the spiritual world. The old instinctive feminine, seen in the power of the Minotaur, needed to be overcome; and the higher feminine needed to await a fuller development of individual consciousness in order to truly awaken. *

In the many pictures which the Greeks had of the gods, they experienced memories of cosmic evolution, but in a much more shadowy way than was the case for the earlier Egypto-Chaldean peoples. Rudolf Steiner refers to the earlier eastern Mystery Temples as the "earthly Guest Houses of the Gods", where the priests and worshippers experienced the actual presence of the divine beings. [42] But for the Greeks, this was different. They felt themselves more united with the earth, with physical, sense-based reality; and in their mysteries they experienced only after-images of the gods. According to Steiner: "The Greek had the feeling: There are indeed Gods, but for man it is only possible to have pictures of these Gods, just as we have in our memory pictures of past experiences, no longer the experiences themselves." [43]

It is in Greek times that we find the real beginnings of written history. This became necessary as human beings could no longer receive a living sense of history through direct experience in the mysteries. Steiner describes the impulse working in Herodotus and those historians who followed him as being "to tear mankind away from the Divine-Spiritual and to set him down in the purely earthly". [44] Humanity was no longer to sit in the lap of the gods and goddesses, but to stand up and develop new strength, and the possibility of new human responsibility.

Gradually a sense of individual identity was incarnating into humanity. Priestly wisdom was giving way to individual human knowledge. Great teachers like Pythagorus (582-507 B.C.) journeyed to diverse mystery centres, and out of their collected experiences founded schools where the old mystery wisdom was brought to life in

* The name 'Ariadne' was given to our work because although Ariadne needed to 'sleep' while the hero – that masculine force for individualization within us all – became stronger, it is now time for her to awaken and take up her life-giving thread in full consciousness. In the myth, when she does awaken to discover Theseus has deserted her, she at first grieves, but in time recovers and goes on to marry the God Dionysus, which proves to be a more fulfilling and lasting union.

new ways. Edouard Schuré states that in the teachings of Pythagorus "we find a rational reproduction of the esoteric doctrine of India and Egypt, to which he gave clarity and Hellenic simplicity, adding a more forceful feeling and a more exact idea of human freedom."[45]

The developing sense of individuality was greatly encouraged in the Greek academies. These schools fostered a more masculine attitude of separation by strengthening the newly awakening capacity for intellectual questioning of all previously accepted assumptions. Like Pythagorus, Plato too had travelled widely and experienced the Mysteries before founding his Academy in Athens. Schuré speaks of Plato's idealism as "a bold affirmation of the divine truths by the soul, which in its solitude questions itself and judges celestial realities by its own intimate faculties and its inner voices."[46] In the Dialogues, Plato transformed esoteric doctrine into human philosophy, and grounded it on a new rationality. In the figure of Socrates we can experience a being who acts completely out of his own sense of truth and who challenges his followers to look within themselves, rather than to rely on traditional moral teachings.

Plato's idealism is made even more earthly, more logical and intellectually formed by Aristotle. Throughout the development of philosophy in classical Greece it is possible to trace the gradual emergence of human understanding from an instinctual, living relationship with the spiritual world toward an ever greater reliance on abstractions, perceived not by grace but by the development of individual human faculties.

Sometimes events in history seem too 'coincidental' to allow an explanation of chance to be very convincing. Such is the case in the 4th century B.C., with the burning of the ancient Mystery Centre at Ephesus on the same day that Alexander the Great was born.[47] The Great Goddess Artemis was the central figure of the Ephesian Mysteries, the last of the Eastern mysteries of the Greeks. The destruction of the Centre heralded the end of the ancient form of mystery teaching and marked the transition out of humanity's identification with the Great Goddess as a revelation of cosmic wisdom. From this same time would arise the individuality of Alexander the Great, who would be remembered for his many conquests and heroic accomplishments, and for the force of his human personality.

The Greek dramatists too recorded the final defeat of the matriarchal consciousness through their treatment of the ancient myths. In describing their portrayal of the story of Orestes, Robert Graves says that the playwrights Aeschylus and Euripides were "writing religious propaganda: Orestes' absolution records the final triumph of the patriarchy."[48] Orestes had killed his mother Clytaemnestra to avenge the murder of his father Agamemnon. In matriarchal times, matricide was the most evil crime imaginable; and so Orestes was hounded by the Erinyes, the Fates, for this unnatural act. At the trial, however, he was acquitted by the Goddess Athene – who significantly had no mother but sprang forth from the head of Zeus. Her final vote upheld the wishes of Apollo and proclaimed the new patriarchal order. As the Greek people experienced the dramas, such pictures worked deeply into their souls and confirmed in them the loosening of the ties of blood and the end of the rule of the Mother.

It seems appropriate to the birth of a new ego force, to the growth of the individual as a differentiated being, that there was such an emphasis on the friendships between men in Greek times. I know that I have learned much about what a renewed feminine force might be, through the support of my women friends. I can imagine that men in Greek times were also experimenting with and learning together about the new, more masculine qualities which were coming to birth within their souls. With our modern emphasis on the physical body, we can place great importance on the aspect of homosexual love in Greek times; but it seems to me that it was not the physical expression of love which was most significant. Rather I see these relationships as attempts at a new kind of genuine meeting, between individualities who for the first time experienced themselves as quite separated beings.

That is, of course, not to imply that Greeks did not value the physical plane. As their consciousness became ever more linked with sense-based perception, they came to deeply appreciate the material world. Their architecture and sculpture are indicative of the reverence with which they lived in the physical reality, while at the same time they reflect their continued experience of space as a living spiritual force. Although the connection was dimming, the Greeks had not yet lost a sense for the divine within the material. They could sculpt the human body so magnificently because they still saw it as incorporating the spirit. As Rudolf Steiner describes it: "The marble of their sculptures took on the appearance of life. The Greek expressed in the physical what lived in his spiritual. Among the Greeks the marriage of the spiritual with the physical was a fact."[49]

Earlier I spoke of how Rudolf Steiner describes the gradual evolution of human consciousness as an emergence out of the total union with, and control by, the spiritual world. I mentioned how he identifies various cultural epochs, and I expressed the idea that in what he calls the Egypto-Chaldean period we can begin to see reflections of the polarity between feminine and masculine as an aspect of the development of human consciousness. The next period he describes is the Greco-Latin. In Greece, human beings found a new relationship to the material world and began to value a new human knowledge in place of the ancient wisdom as revealed through the priests. But it is in the Roman phase of this Greco-Latin cultural epoch that reason and logic really begin to hold sway over revelation and intuition.

Descent into Matter

The Romans devised their laws and institutions according to their own, human requirements. Justice was no longer determined through the expression of divine commandments. Individual rights became important when human beings began experiencing themselves as independent entities:

"The concept of the citizen first became a real feeling in ancient Rome. By that time man had brought the spiritual into the physical world as far as his own individuality. The last Will and Testament was invented in ancient Rome. The will of the single personality had become so strong that even beyond death it could determine what should be done with its property, its own things. The single personal man was now the determining factor."[50]

Significantly, the Roman citizens were referred to as 'patricians' from the Latin word 'pater', meaning father. As the masculine influence took a firmer hold in individuals and in the culture, as the feeling for individual responsibility expanded, the sense of separation from the gods grew even stronger. The Roman gods became increasingly abstract and utilitarian, their services were catalogued and bought, and the celebrations of ancient rites degenerated into empty ritual. Humanity was descending more and more into materialization and individualization, and going further away from any genuinely experienced connection to the spiritual world.

It was during this Greco-Latin epoch, during this period of humanity's descent into matter, that the being of Christ incarnated on the earth. Rudolf Steiner speaks in many places of the profound significance of this event at this particular time in human history. The Greeks had so permeated matter with the spirit that they could represent the gods in their own human images. The Romans further strengthened the sense of being an individual personality on this earth, but even they never entirely lost a connection to the spirit. Nevertheless, according to Steiner, if humanity was to avoid descending too deeply into the confines of the material world, the appearance of Christ at just this time was "positively necessary in the whole spiritual course of human events." Steiner elaborates this further:

"Christianity could arise only at a time when men were not yet so deeply immersed in matter that they were likely to over-estimate its worth; when they were not yet plunged so deeply into matter as is the case in our age, but were still able to spiritualize it and to penetrate it."[51]

Christ brought to humanity the possibility of a new ascent of the spirit out of matter; through his resurrection he conquered physical death and made conceivable the rebirth of the spirit within each individual. The older ways by which human beings could feel connected to the divine world, could partake in the cosmic wisdom, were no longer appropriate: "When man became a personality, God also had to become a personality in order to save him, to give him the possibility of rising again."[52]

Humanity was becoming more and more divided, as evidenced in the loosening of the older, maternal, tribal blood ties. To this necessary differentiation, Christ brought the seed of a new, now spiritual re-connection. Through His impulse, the separating, developing egos of humanity acquired the possibility of understanding the relationship between individual destiny and participation in the totality. As Steiner expresses it: "Christ was to represent to humanity the great pattern of a being who had established within himself harmony and concord between his Ego and the maternal principle."[53]

Whatever one's religious persuasion, I think the being of Christ can be universally recognized as an image of great harmony. In the redemptive power of His Love lies an active inner balancing of feminine and masculine qualities. In considering this inner balance, I think we can have some inkling of the essence of that far future androgynous state of humanity referred to earlier in this chapter. Occasionally great artists have captured this premonition in their portrayals of Christ. The beautiful sketch of the 'Head of Christ' by Leonardo da Vinci, done in preparation for the painting of 'The Last Supper', depicts a truly androgynous face – it is not just a man, nor a woman, but somehow both in all their fullness, and therefore more.

Christ's life on earth unfolded as the fulfillment of the prophesies of the Hebrew patriarchs. These highly evolved beings had been contributing to the development of human consciousness by organizing their people within a strong patriarchal tradition. They sought to resist the decadent, matriarchal, pagan influences around them by emphasizing the supreme authority and command of the Father God; and they portrayed Eve as the temptress in an effort to subdue the importance of the feminine forces. The Old Testament, as a revelation of cosmic evolution, reveals their more masculine intentions in its abstract conceptions. As Rudolf Steiner expresses it: "There the essence was lifted out of the direct living experience and became doctrine, theory. This was necessary, for only so could mankind be led – and that is the meaning of the Old Testament – be led from that living in union with the outer world, which still had an inner connection with the microcosm, man, and the macrocosm, the world, to their further evolution."[54]

The Judaeo-Christian tradition in Western civilization reflects many aspects of 'masculine striving', in spite of its apparent dependence on faith and revelation and the more feminine 'priestly wisdom'. Christ's own harmony was a seed for development; after his incarnation, human beings continued to go even further into materialism. And this was necessary if we were to develop as true individualities, as self-conscious and responsible ego-beings. We may question today if we have perhaps gone too far, if in fact we have become slaves of matter and have forgotten to nurture the seed of spiritual renewal; but it is in the possibility of even asking this question that we can know something of our potential for human freedom. If humanity had never become separated from the gods, if it had not been declared that "God is dead", we would not be able, as independent beings, to seek for new understanding of the non-physical dimensions of our reality. Nor would we be able, freely and consciously, to open within ourselves a sense of responsibility for the furthering of evolution.

This jumps ahead of our historical perspective. In fact, I do not intend to look chronologically at the last 2,000 years of human history. As it is, I have skimmed through long ages, only picking out moments, images of feminine and masculine along the path of evolving consciousness. In the time since Christ, the interweaving of feminine and masculine forces has all too often fallen into the realm of struggle between men and women. It has been a time of growing masculine influence, and many of the ways of fostering this influence have been far from subtle – especially from a woman's point of view. Not only feminine qualities and ways of being, but also women themselves, have been increasingly repressed and limited in their possibilities as mankind has pushed its way toward objectivity, discipline and control over physical reality. Much recent women's literature has dealt with the many manifestations of this oppression of women. I only want to suggest the trend, the movement away from valuing the feminine, away from respecting and nurturing an intuitive, imaginative, holistic approach to all of life.

In so many spheres it is possible to see how the identification of women and the feminine led to a rigidifying of tasks within sex-based roles. In ancient times women fulfilled a variety of functions; but gradually as jobs became more professional, women were replaced by men as farmers, bakers, cooks, crafts'men'. The transition from mid-wife or herbal healer to doctor is a clear example of the male assumption of authority. Not only were women excluded from their former roles, but these essentially rhythmical tasks have become ever more efficient, mechanical and sterile under the masculine influence.

The development of Christianity, and certainly the treatment of women by the Church, offer much evidence of the ever-growing power of the masculine. Although the priests continued to rely on inspiration for the revelation of cosmic truths, the early Church 'Fathers' created a rigidly patriarchal structure for the Catholic Church, with many restrictions placed on women. The growth of the Church, strongly rooted as it was in Roman tradition, gives a picture of an institution becoming ever more earthly, ever less divine. Not surprisingly, with the development of Protestantism we find a decrease in the significance of the Madonna as an image of the Great Mother. This being of divine wisdom, who could bear Christ, was stripped of her essential power of inspiration.

Right up to the present it is possible to trace the gradual decline of art, imagination and spiritual vision as revealed in church buildings and services. The old forms of worship no longer speak to people's soul needs, and the new 'reforms' in many churches too often mirror the materialistic tendencies of the rest of society. I am sure individual priests of all denominations yearn for new spiritual vision and for new ways to reach modern men and women, but I am often saddened by the methods they employ. The parish church in the village where I lived in England suffered from a lack of active worshippers; so weekly slogans were put on a billboard in front of the church to attract interest. In the process, religion became a commodity to be sold like beer – "Jesus reaches parts others cannot reach" – or merely an imitation of television clichés – "Who loves ya' baby? – God does."

The difficult struggle in recent years within the Anglican (Episcopal) Church over the acceptance of women as priests – to say nothing of the refusal by the leadership of the Roman Catholic Church even to take the question seriously – is a clear example of the state of confusion in modern people about questions of feminine and masculine. Many churches have become increasingly masculine in their vision – this was of course necessary if people were to develop into responsible individuals free from the dictates of the spiritual world. But now too many church leaders appear unable to look toward further development or to see the need for a new opening out of feminine qualities through individual conscious decision. Of course individual men and women must seek – and in fact are seeking – this opening out; but it is symptomatic of the narrowness of vision to which the masculine can go, that so many priests and ministers reject women in their unconscious fear of the changes a new valuing of the feminine might bring. If, like the Amazons of old, church leaders entrench themselves in a defensive stance, they, and their empty churches, may be left behind in the advancement of human consciousness.

Rudolf Steiner refers to the present epoch of human development, this period which has followed after the Greco-Latin times, as the age of the Conciousness Soul. In characterizing this age, he describes an intensification of the awareness of duality within the human soul. On the one hand, we have experienced an ever greater interest and ability in exploring the sense-perceptible world, in conquering physical reality through the force of will and the intellect. This is connected to the masculine inclination which has been such a dominant factor in the development of science and technology as we know them today. Through this side of ourselves, we have grown in objectivity, scientific detachment, self-discipline and rationality; and our knowledge about the facts of material reality has burgeoned into even broader fields. And still, there is that other side of the duality within us: that part which yearns toward the spirit, toward unity with others, that more feminine aspect which has been gradually put into the background in both society and in individuals. We have grown in our awareness of personal identity; but as the scale has tipped ever more to this one side, we have come to feel isolated, cut off from each other, estranged from both nature and the spirit. This loneliness and alienation is a fundamental experience of the Consciousness Soul age. Yet as we evolve into the future, the question is whether we can reach out of our private worlds and find new ways of meeting, new forms of working together responsibly within the whole of the cosmos. Will we be able, by working with our developing sense of selfhood, to consciously seek for a creative balancing of the duality of our human existence?

Quests for Wholeness

Let us look at our present situation in society for signs of an intention toward greater balance, for indications of movement out of the isolation, rigidity and role-encased superficiality which are so much a part of modern life. But first I want to take one last glance backward, to search for threads of potential balance which have been weaving within the general trend of masculine influence over the last few thousand years. The dream of balance has never been completely submerged; in addition to the inspiration for spiritual renewal in the figure of Christ, there also have been other related imaginations and movements encouraging humanity, however subtly, toward a more harmonious future.

Historically there have been moments when pictures of balance have emerged out of the folk imagination, have even been symbolically manifested in some spheres of everyday life. For example, in the stories of the Grail, people could experience the potential wholeness of human nature and could find models for their own behaviour. Through the many images – of the knight's quest, of the women bearing the Grail cup, of love as the source of inspiration and spiritual fulfillment – people in the Middle Ages could imagine the possibility of human harmony. With the rise of Chivalry, there was a tremendous glorification of loyalty, strength and courage – as masculine virtues – and of piety, beauty and gentleness – as feminine virtues. Dreadfully stereotyped definitions from our modern perspective, but nevertheless powerful images which, however ideal, contributed to a time of great creativity and flourishing in the arts. As a part of their glorification of the ideal feminine, the troubadours, and also certain orders within the Church, worshipped Mary as the Queen of Heaven and sought her as a mediator to spiritual experience, as a bridge to God.

Other strands interweaving toward some eventual balance of feminine and masculine forces can be found in various occult groups. The phenomena of men's secret societies, and in particular the development of Free Masonry is revealing. Originally the Free Masons were an esoteric order with the intention of aiding in the birth of the Ego within the human individuality. The order has roots reaching as far back as ancient Egypt and Greece. Through the mystery rituals, the men underwent a kind of initiation; they experienced a spiritual rebirth. Women were always excluded because the feminine element was considered dangerous to the development of the masculine energy needed for individual identity.

To view this fostering of masculine energy within all-male groupings as a positive force toward human balance requires us to remember the general context of a lingering, and from a certain point of view therefore threatening, unconscious feminine relationship to the spirit – even within the Christian Church. Perhaps this appears to contradict what was said above about the masculine nature of Christianity as it has developed. The early Church hierarchy manifested its power in patriarchal ways, through strict authority and doctrine and male leadership; but the relationship to the spirit itself, for priests and laymen, was still of an earlier feminine nature, dependent upon inspiration and unquestioning faith. In this context, the activity of the early Free Masons was an important contribution toward a future personal and conscious relationship to the spirit; one could even say toward the possibility of individual quests for fertilization by the spirit.

But even movements which begin with an occult intention for balance, can in time rigidify into a one-sidedness which belies the original aim. So we can see how Free Masonry has become ever more materialistic and has lost its esoteric task; the rituals have become decadent, the occult significance is forgotten.

There were other occult groups as well who held on, at least for a time, to the threads of a future balance, and so nurtured along humanity's dream of conscious unity. In the practice of Alchemy in the Middle Ages there was clearly an awareness of the need to work with polarity if a truly creative process was to occur. In many paintings of this time, the alchemist is pictured performing his experiments with his wife by his side, a symbolic recognition that masculine and feminine energy are required in any true transformation, whether it is from base metal to gold or as a part of self-development.

Related, partially hidden brotherhoods like the Rosicrucians worked esoterically to understand spiritual truths and so to live and work in greater balance. Modern Rosicrucianism began in the fifteenth century, at the dawn of the age of the Consciousness Soul. It was concerned with developing a knowledge about the spiritual world which was appropriate to the present age with its emphasis on material reality and on the freedom of the individual. Rudolf Steiner describes the Rosicrucian attitude in the following way:

"The Rosicrucian does not consider it his task to withdraw in any way from the physical world. . . For what he has to do is to spiritualize the physical world, especially in the world of men."[55]

Here clearly is a wish to bring balance between the spiritual and the physical dimensions of reality. That wish is not in itself directly parallel to a conscious desire to balance masculine and feminine forces; but it does require individuals to pay some attention to how the masculine and feminine elements manifest and how they can be channeled by each striving person.

More modern occult teachings, such as Theosophy and also Anthroposophy, developed out of a connection to the Rosicrucian path. In speaking about Theosophy in 1905, Rudolf Steiner said that it "was preparing on the spiritual plane what will later happen on the physical plane, the re-unification of the sexes", and he referred to it as "manly-female wisdom".[56] Later Steiner separated himself from the Theosophical Movement; but this aspect of working ever more consciously toward the coming together of feminine and masculine energy, coupled with the presentation of a developmental path clearly available to both men and women, remained an essential aspect of what he developed in Anthroposophy. The name which he gave this science of the spirit reveals the intended balance in the coming together of 'Anthropos', from the Greek word for man, and 'Sophia', the divine feminine imagination of cosmic wisdom.

Looking at quite a different level of human reality it is possible to find another, generally unseen, balancing thread weaving through these years of growing masculine influence. This is the fibre built by the endurance and resilience of the millions of women who have patiently cared for their families, sacrificed their own personal ambitions, and generally nurtured the quality of life forward throughout centuries of external confinement and prejudice. Perhaps this labour was most often done unconsciously; nevertheless a positive feminine force has been working through generations of women, maintaining the fabric of human life, patching the holes left by the advancing masculine stride.

The Women's Movement

Gradually the severe restrictions on personal fulfillment, and the active undervaluing of women and the feminine qualities they embodied, became intolerable for increasing numbers of women. During the eighteenth century in the United States and England in particular, a tide began mounting, fed by the intellectual and moral fervour of the enlightenment and the American War of Independence; it built up through the rationality and social action of the nineteenth century and burst out with the Suffragette Movement, which was finally successful in gaining women the vote at the beginning of this century.

The struggles of women in the twentieth century – for the right to vote, for equal opportunity in employment, for basic dignity and respect – have taken many forms. But always underlying the efforts is the basic assumption that what women are capable of doing should not be determined by men. On this point, in his Philosophy of Freedom, published in 1894, Rudolf Steiner gave a great boost to feminism with the following statement:

"The social position of women is for the most part such an unworthy one because in so many respects it is determined not as it should be by the particular characteristics of the individual woman, but by the general picture one has of her general tasks and needs. A man's activity in life is governed by his individual capacities and inclinations, whereas a woman's is determined by the mere fact that she is a woman. She is supposed to be a slave to what is generic, to womanhood in general. As long as men continue to debate whether a woman is suited to this or that profession 'according to her natural disposition', the so-called woman's question cannot advance beyond its most elementary stage. What a woman, within her natural limitations, wants to become had better be left to the woman herself to decide. If it is true that women are suited only to that profession which is theirs at present, then they will hardly have it in them to attain any other. But they must be allowed to decide for themselves what is in accordance with their nature. To all who fear an upheaval of our social structure through accepting women as individuals and not as females, we must reply that a social structure in which the status of one half of humanity is unworthy of a human being is itself in great need of improvement."[57]

And so it is! But, it is not only the status of one half of humanity which needs improvement; half of our inner being itself – as women and as men – is in desperate need of new value and new possibilities for expression. We can no longer speak of balance unless with consciousness and individual responsibility we try to uncover and make manifest the eternal feminine within us. We must re-awaken and transform this repressed, slumbering aspect of our nature if we will seek to offset the rigidity and materialism of our modern ways, if we will truly work for greater human harmony.

In this context it is not hard to understand the impulse behind the renewed women's movement of the last twenty years: it is clearly a part of a deep human intention for balance. The focus has been on women because women were most obviously suffering the effects of an excessively patriarchal power structure. The threads of patience and endurance have been stretched to their limit and they have snapped. Centuries of unrecognized hurt and anger have burst out of the being – the human being – of womankind. But because modern women are as much a part of the masculine age as men, are as much influenced by the intellectual rationality and aggression which abound in our culture, the women's movement has often seemed to merely echo the times in its methods and its demands.

The development of the movement seems full of paradox; much of what we see or read about it appears antithetical to the feminine as I have been describing it. The ways of some feminists can seem to reflect the least admirable masculine traits of our culture. But how could it be otherwise in our modern world of power play, violence, self-centredness and head-based consciousness? In this societal atmosphere it is not surprising that many feminists match their anger with a logical analysis of the ways women have been treated and then adopt a masculine stance to demand equal rights.

The plea for equality in the political and economical sphere is valid and vital, but it is not the only answer to the struggling relationship between men and women today; and it can fail to recognize the perhaps greater need for relationship between the feminine and masculine within each individual and within the whole of our social life.

Our modern methods of education and interaction have greatly encouraged the development of masculine qualities in both men and women. Women often find themselves caught in an inner turmoil of mixed values. Educated to be rational, independent, and articulate they are somehow also expected to be self-sacrificing, submissive, and nurturing. The mixed expectations come not only from without, but from deep within as well. Men too, increasingly experience confusion about how to manifest their more gentle, caring sides without losing prestige in our masculine-orientated culture. The women's movement has done much to bring this confusion into discussion; more and more people today are aware of how they have been channelled into roles by their upbringing, are freeing themselves from simplistic definitions as 'woman' or 'man', and are experimenting with the various sides of their natures. Nevertheless, as valuable as this discussion and experimentation is, it is still generally dominated by a masculine set of values; and the expressed goals are most often greater personal power, and autonomy, and effectiveness in the material world.

Too many women today forget their very apt analysis of the problems in society in their efforts to be accepted as equals in the social structure as it is. If we recognize the serious shortcomings of our society, we face the challenge to not merely share in furthering the status quo, but much more importantly to consciously develop and foster what is so urgently needed in all our modern social forms and interactions: a renewed feminine force. It is vitally important that more and more women are able to enter all levels of the work force; but it is not only the personal fulfillment of individual women that is at stake. The women moving into new positions of responsibility in so many fields are a tremendous potential force for change – change in the ways and atmosphere of working, and change in the results and products of the work as well.

A woman's right to do what she feels called to do in the world is only one side of the question; the other side is with what responsibility she enters into what she does. It seems to me that as we grow ever more self-conscious, ever freer from the external dictates of gods and men, we cannot speak of rights without responsibilities. If we will talk collectively of women's rights, then must we not also consider collectively women's responsibilities?

Like so many movements before it, the women's movement runs the risk of becoming one-sided in an excessive emphasis on the question of rights. When it is most strident in this direction, it arouses equally one-sided defensive reaction or sentimental backlash – from men and from women. In the long run, to get lost in this kind of aggressive-defensive battle would be a sad digression from an essential impulse in human development and a tragic entrapment within the materialistic perspective of our modern consciousness. As the initial anger and aggression accomplish some of the necessary breakthroughs in external barriers, I hope that the women's movement will be able to build a broad enough base to encourage a whole range of changes in individuals and in our social forms, will be able to encompass seemingly disparate elements with basic good will. Otherwise I fear it will fall prey to the dominance and ultimate control of our fragmented, narrow-visioned age. To retain this breadth of vision and be truly encompassing, the women's movement will need to recognize and foster ever more consciously the responsibility which modern women can assume in bringing a renewed feminine quality into the development of humanity as a whole.

Just as I know that within me are my own particular, and ever changing, feminine and masculine qualities, so also I feel sure that there are reasons why at this time in history I live in a woman's body; and I feel a special bond with other women, a kind of shared quest to understand fully and enact more carefully our collective responsibilities within the whole of humanity. I have come to feel that as women, we have within us – built even into our female bodies – a kind of universal storehouse of feminine qualities and sensitivities. But these have been overlaid throughout centuries, and perhaps also more specifically in our own education, by a heavy residue of masculine influence and development. The time has now come when we need to penetrate these layers to uncover what lies deep within us. In no way do I think we should, or even could, deny the masculine qualities that are a part of us; rather we must use them in a new way to discover and help transform the feminine possibilities within us so that we may evolve toward a more truly human balance.

In her chapter, Margli Matthews deals more specifically with the challenge within each individual to awaken an active feminine force. I want only to suggest that in our actual experiences as women we can find seeds of understanding, possibilities of recognition, and encouragement toward better meeting the needs of the times. For example, modern life is incredibly a-rhythmic, to the extent that in America it is common to find all night, seven-day-a-week shopping. We extend our working hours to include breakfast, lunch and supper meetings; we fix ancient yearly festivals on Mondays no matter when they really fall; and in the process, we rob ourselves of any sense of the connection between our being and the rhythms of the sun, moon and stars. But if as women we could value the lunar rhythm which manifests in our bodies each month in the menstrual cycle, if we could learn from this something of the very nature and purpose of rhythm and of humanity's place within the whole of the cosmos, then we could perhaps contribute to a more enlivened sense of the wholeness and meaning of each day, a week, a year or a lifetime.

So much of our modern consciousness, so many of our daily decisions, reside in the head, in dry abstract facts and hardened differentiation; but if we will discover living images and breathing relationships in the world around us, then we must expand our consciousness out of the confines of the head and into the realm of the heart as well. Then our understanding might begin to pulse and flow with cosmic rhythm and wisdom. In most aspects of social life today there is a fair amount of head consciousness – we have an over-abundance of ideas and theories about everything. In addition there is a good deal of active will power at work – Americans in particular have always been known as real 'doers'. But often the heart which should connect head and will is cramped and underdeveloped; then our thoughts and our actions run all the more rampantly in their separate directions. Significantly, heart disease is a major killer.

There is great need in our times to develop what Rudolf Steiner frequently refers to as heart thinking, and for me this is connected to a renewal of feminine qualities within the human soul. Traditionally women have recognized the heart's needs and responded to its rhythms, have nurtured the feeling sphere in social life. It cannot be insignificant that the heart was eclipsed by the head and the will in a time of masculine influence, a time when women's possibilities were severely circumscribed.

The challenge now is to develop a new kind of heart consciousness which can form a living bridge between our thoughts and our actions, which can become a truly creative social force for human development. But as Steiner emphasizes in a lecture entitled *How can the psychological distress of today be overcome?* "The impulses for a new way of working in the world will have to be won consciously from the heart's blood. What will happen of its own accord is the estrangement of individuals from one another. What will flow from the human heart has to be sought consciously."[58] Without consciousness the heart runs the risk of becoming sentimental; we all know how easy it is to get lost in heart-throbs and heart-aches, in an endless swirl of emotional feelings. But can we take hold of our individual ego strength and with it go consciously into the feeling sphere? Then perhaps we shall be able to listen more carefully to our heart's message, hear our inner voices and develop the courage to act in accordance with them.

Obviously this is a challenge for both women and men today. But it is the feminine in us all which can be receptive to the heart's messages, open to the spirit's call. Like the mother who hears her child whimpering in the night through closed doors, a consciously renewed feminine force could create a heart sensitivity capable of awakening to the real needs of modern life. The old, instinctive feminine will no longer do, for it shuns consciousness and in so doing its receptivity can devour and its protection can smother. What is now required is an active, enheartening caring, a transformed life-giving sense of rhythm and unity, and a new, freely developed trust in the heart and spirit of humanity.

The New Feminine

In many spheres of modern life it is possible to see a renewed feminine awareness gradually emerging in the consciousness of women and men. I have already referred to the women's movement, but there are several other recent concerns as well which indicate the far-reaching impulse for greater balance today. The interest in ecology, for example, focuses on the value of the wholeness of the earth, rather than on the endless exploitation of her parts. Gradually people are beginning to question the necessity of the many meaningless, death-oriented products which flood the modern marketplace and pollute the atmosphere through their means of production or because they cannot waste away within any natural cycle of decay. Slowly we are becoming aware of the importance of caring for the earth's natural resources and of restoring the organic balances in air, water and soil. As with all modern dilemmas, we walk a tightrope between wanting to return to the mother's womb in a complete anti-technology, back-to-the-earth approach, and wanting to be masters of nature, overlords who can regulate all things and even create life in a laboratory. Always there is the challenge to use the individualized consciousness and technical knowledge we have developed over long ages, in ways which respect the world we are a part of and make us worthy co-workers with the gods.

I see the growing interest in organic and bio-dynamic farming as an expression of a feminine impulse as well. Here is a wish consciously to re-connect to cosmic rhythms, to nurture the soil, and to provide the real needs of human nutrition. For many years the food we eat has been analyzed, pulverized, processed and refortified in the interests of greater convenience, 'improved' flavour, and of course economic profit. In the process, food production has become ever more mechanized, and human beings have lost the innate instinct for what really nourishes. Now, out of the vacuum of the pre-packaged man-made wonders, people are beginning to look more consciously at what role food plays in human life and growth – not just vitamin enrichment, but real, tasty, natural foodstuff. As more people recognize the need for wholesome food, its preparation – whether in the field or in the kitchen – must receive greater respect and support. Happily this is beginning to occur. As it does, plants, animals, soil and water will surely all benefit from more responsible and caring human handling; and human beings too, will grow more healthy and more whole.

In the medical sphere in recent years there has also been a movement for a more holistic approach to health care; and this too, I think, shows the feminine concern for the total person. It has grown in response to the emphasis in modern medicine on treating the isolated symptom, on removing the slightest discomfort as quickly and as painlessly as possible, and on treating the patient all too often as primarily a statistic for scientific research. Gradually more and more people are beginning to question the long term effects of this dehumanizing approach, are beginning to recognize that body and soul are not separated entities and that real healing does not mean bolstering the physical body along with drugs and external props, but involves strengthening the individuality within the body so that it can better resist, or if need be accept, its own difficulties, as a part of its own particular development.

In the social sphere there are many indications of a growing feminine awareness and wish for a more inward sense of unity between people. Since the Sixties there has been a particularly intense questioning on a wide scale of the social forms which have traditionally bound people together but which now appear to be crumbling. In the face of so much social fragmentation, more and more people are struggling for new kinds of relationships – no longer so defined by external roles as in the past, but built on a commitment to share a path of mutual development. There have been many attempts at new forms of community, experiments in living and working with others in new ways, not because of blood ties but out of a conscious desire to discover together ways of caring and interacting which bridge our individual experiences of isolation and self-orientation. Humanity has a long way to go before real community built on conscious and heartfelt commitment to the needs of others is commonplace; but the efforts being made today are vital, however they may 'fail' by our present judgments of success. Within the souls of men, women and children striving to bring about more living social forms, new possibilities of compassion, and selflessness, and responsibility to the totality are slowly taking root.

Groups of all kinds provide the soil for many modern interactions. Often with painful self-consciousness, people come together in group settings to explore new ways of meeting others and to learn from others more about themselves. It seems inevitable that the growth of consciousness involves pain; what is so interesting to me is that as modern people we have developed the concept of the group as a place where individuals can be held and encouraged by others to grow through this pain. There have been many illusions and false expectations in the development of group work as a source of greater self and social awareness; nevertheless the continuing interest in and commitment to the possibilities of group efforts indicate the basic human wish to overcome the excessive separation and selfishness in our modern life.

A kind of group which took on special significance in the sixties and seventies is the women's group. Earlier I suggested that fundamental to the growth of the women's movement was a recognition of the need to renew the feminine as a balancing force in society. I see the coming together of women in groups as contributing not only to the development of self-confidence, assertiveness and political awareness, but perhaps even more importantly, as allowing women to awaken, with growing consciousness, the slumbering feminine qualities so needed today. Hopefully the raised consciousness of women does not get stuck at the political level, but can work as an enheartening, balancing force at all levels of social life.

I wonder if the phenomena of women's groups is a kind of parallel development to the earlier separation into men's secret societies where the birth of the human ego could be aided by the masculine sense of individuality. Now, women are creating together situations in which a transformed feminine force can be allowed to develop. Many women feel the need to work in groups without men – at least for a time – in order to explore a more feminine way of interacting without being criticized for a lack of discipline or the absence of a clearly defined goal. By trusting in the free flow of intuitions, feelings and imaginations – while still struggling to control excessive chattiness – women are finding new ways to achieve aims and are developing a sense for movement which is not logically preordained but which grows out of the substance of the common work. Hopefully the need for separation will subside as feminine qualities are more valued and more actively developed by both women and men.

The following poem was written by a woman in a mixed group I was once a part of when we were exploring the challenge for the feminine today. The men in the group wanted the women to be clearer about what we were doing, they wanted to know what exactly were women going on about. The poem was written to them; but it just as well expresses the inner battle we all can experience between our detached, observing masculine side which wants clear-cut answers, and that more elusive, evolving feminine which seeks to trust in the unknown and gently receive what it barely begins to intuite.

> *Masculine, Feminine?*
> You sit back to front
> On your chair
> Arms resting on the back
> Abstracted
> Keeping your distance –
> Lest a stray feeling
> Draw you in unprepared.
> We, struggling with formless beginnings,
> Sit in an uneasy circle
> Not knowing what would be born –
> Or whether words
> Can carry it.
>
> Sylvia Mehta

Through my participation in a variety of women's groups I have experienced a gradual re-valuation and re-education of the feminine in me. I have learned much about the nature of caring, and acceptance, and vulnerability. I have been able to observe, and to practise, manifestations of the feminine which had been quite underdeveloped in my everyday life. I have felt the active, heartwarming support of others in my struggles at self-development and have tried to encourage others along their particular paths as well. I have learned to appreciate the wonderful complexity and variety of life experiences, to respect the uniqueness of each one's path, and yet to feel the unity of our common human striving.

Traditionally we have the image of the mother holding her child to her heart and nourishing it toward its future. But in our age, if society is not to rigidify in cold functionalism, women and men must actively strive to carry not only children, but one another as well, in the warmth of their hearts. Conscious attention to the feminine in us can foster a genuine heart-carrying, which neither wishes to possess others nor to force them into abstract molds, but which believes in and lends support to the developing ego being within us all. We need to find ways to recognize the levels of our human interdependency, and then with reverence and responsibility be true to our intentions of mutual development.

But, of course, people today are so afraid of needing others. To be strong is to be independent, self-sufficient, in control; to show vulnerability is to be weak, a sissy, 'unmanly'. In many women's groups and other self-awareness groups as well, these definitions have been challenged. People are beginning to look more consciously at their feelings and their needs, are trying to be true to an inner sense of what is right for them, and are struggling to overcome the fear of rejection or ridicule if they differ slightly from society's accepted norms. It is the feminine in us which lets us show our vulnerability. This can be done inadvertently, out of a state of crisis, or as an act of inner courage, trusting that others can and will bring understanding and help. To consciously share one's doubts and worries or one's less than perfect sides, to let down the facade of being in absolute control, can open the way to undreamed-of possibilities for relationship and growth. Hopefully the effort to be more open and to trust in others which is being exercised in a variety of group situations can be extended into social life generally. This would serve as such an antidote to the fear and isolation which abound today, and could foster a renewed sense of unity between individuals and an enlivened experience of the spirit working in all humanity.

I have tried to point to a few of the many social concerns today where people are struggling to develop a more imaginative, rhythmic, unifying and enlivening force to meet the rationality, order, differentiation and technological know-how of our modern age. In so many ways we can feel the impulse for greater balance working into our lives; from all directions we catch glimpses of a potential future unity. But because we are so rooted in a sense-based consciousness, we hardly know how to receive or work with these inklings of spiritual truth. Often we try quickly to materialize them – in fashions or laws or social custom: We sense our future human androgyny and so adopt a unisex style in clothes and hair, forgetting that a real uni-form can only evolve out of a conscious inner balancing of feminine and masculine; we define equal opportunity in job hours and pay packets but neglect to see the meaning in each individual's growth in the variety of human possibilities; we value self-fulfillment and personal flexibility and so avoid long-term relationships, only to remain desperately alone, deprived of the growth which comes through commitment and actively shared responsibility. In our modern desire for immediate tangible results we all too easily ignore the call for long-term conscious inner development which belongs to any impulse for individual growth, or balance, or unity with others. Then we run the risk of pinning down into rigid forms that which needs careful tending at a variety of levels if it would be encouraged to full flowering.

But how can we responsibly approach the new thresholds of awareness, the new possibilities of relationship with others, or the new calls to social activity which present themselves on all fronts? How can we avoid the pitfalls of premature materialization, cold functionalism, or vain self-importance? Of course such questions have no simple answers; as modern people we can only struggle on, trying to meet the challenges of each day as consciously as possible. But if we can come to know the non-physical as well as the physical dimensions of our reality, if we can actively believe in every individual's potential for development, and especially if we can carry in our hearts a living image of the human being, then surely we will be more attentive to the real needs of the present age.

So we come again to the need to renew the feminine as a balancing force in individuals and in society. A pregnant woman, in her role as embodied feminine, carries the incarnating child within her until it is ready to be born, able to emerge into its independent existence. Today all people, women and men, are called upon to hold and nurture within them, that which humanity would become. In the face of this challenge, I find it so interesting that there has been such attention given to the process of pregnancy and childbirth in recent years. More and more women are seeking to be conscious of what is going on in their bodies, are wanting to enter into the natural rhythms of what is happening, and are resisting the pressures to be put to sleep during the birth.

Any process of birth takes time, and it requires our patience as well as our energy. It is heartening to see how many women are beginning to resist the pressure to induce birth out of respect for a more essential timing than hospital convenience.

In any birth things become more difficult if you fight what is coming, easier if you can go with the process in consciousness. This latter involves dealing with any accompanying discomfort, accepting it as a part of the whole event. There may be times in the process when you feel anxious, or even a bit ridiculous – you must pant and push, and you may not get the timing just right, so you may push when you should hold. But you still go on, through the fear and the uncertainty, believing that what is coming is right, trying to carry with reverence and joy, an image of the being on its way.

I feel that this picture of the attention and activity being brought to the process of natural childbirth captures something of the effort to renew the feminine today. Certainly there have been instances in the development of the women's movement when the timing has seemed off: there have been attempts to induce, sometimes an excess of pushing, and even threats of miscarriage of the basic impulse; but underlying all the difficulties of the labour has been a powerful faith in the human potential and a keen desire to create a more balanced future. Although the pain involved is sometimes intense, there is no going back, nor any longer the possibility of sleeping through, or of ignoring that something is trying to emerge into human consciousness. To extend the image slightly further, it is encouraging to see how many men today are coming out of the stereotype of the detached father and are wanting to be present at the birth of their children, actively supporting the mother and consciously facilitating the process of birth. In the picture of natural childbirth, both parents, as representatives of feminine and masculine, work together to welcome what is wanting to be born through their union. Women have encouraged men to enter the world of childbirth, and men have been enlivened by the experience.

We have many things to bring to birth today. An activated feminine awareness can help us carry and nurture a true image of our human potential, can enhearten the masculine energy in us all, and can invite a more balanced participation of feminine and masculine at all levels of our human experience. Then as women and as men we may become more conscious of the inter-working of spirit and matter in our development and so be more able to responsibly open ourselves to ever new dimensions of creativity. With appreciation for our experience of polarity on earth we may then move forward together on the long path of human liberation.

Footnotes

1. Rudolf Steiner, *Cosmic Memory, Prehistory of Earth and Man,* 1 West Nyack, New York: Rudolf Steiner Publications Inc., 1959.

2. Ibid., p.87.

3. Rudolf Steiner, *The Theosophy of the Rosicrucians,* London: Rudolf Steiner Press 1966, p.141.

4. Ibid., p.148.

5. Steiner, *Cosmic Memory,* p.90.

6. Rudolf Steiner, *Occult Science, An Outline,* London: Rudolf Steiner Press, 1963.

7. Rudolf Steiner, "Freimaurerei und Menschheitsentwickelung" in *Die Tempellegende und die Goldene Legende,* Dornach: Rudolf Steiner Verlag 1979, pp.228 – 242.

8. Steiner, *Cosmic Memory,* p.88.

9. Steiner, "Freimaurerei...", p.231.

10. Ibid.

11. Mircea Eliade, *Gods, Goddesses and Myths of Creation,* New York: Harper and Row, 1974, p.98.

12. Robert Graves, *The Greek Myths: I,* Penguin Books, 1960, p.27.

13. Ibid., p.31.

14. Helen Diner, *Mothers and Amazons,* New York: Anchor Books, 1973, p.11.

15. Graves, p.13.

16. Steiner, *Cosmic Memory,* p.74.

17. Ibid., p.73.

18. Ibid., p.78.

19. Ibid., p.80.

20. Rudolf Steiner, *True and False Paths of Spiritual Investigation*, London: Rudolf Steiner Press, 1969, p.35.

21. J. J. Bachofen, *Myth, Religion and Mother Right*, Princeton: Bolingen Series LXXXIV, 1973, p.71.

22. James Mellaart, *Catal Hüyük*, London, Thames and Hudson, 1976.

23. An interesting book, published since this chapter was written, which discusses the influence of the feminine and early women on cultural evolution is: *The Time Falling Bodies Take to Light*, William Irwin Thompson, New York: St Martin's Press 1981.

24. Steiner, "Freimaurerei...", p.230.

25. Eliade, p.106.

26. Erich Neumann, *The Origins and History of Consciousness*, Princeton: Bolingen Series XLII, 1970, pp.39 – 40.

27. Rudolf Steiner, *Egyptian Myths and Mysteries*, New York: Anthroposophic Press Inc., 1971, p.69.

28. Ibid., p.8.

29. Neumann, p.64.

30. Diner, p.173.

31. Steiner, *Egyptian Myths and Mysteries*, p.93.

32. Several of the books by Steiner quoted so far contain descriptions of the different cultural epochs, in particular: *Occult Science; Egyptian Myths and Mysteries; The Theosophy of the Rosicrucians*.

33. Steiner, *Occult Science*, p.211.

34. Padraic Colum, *Myths of the World*, New York: The Universal Library, 1972, p.19.

35. Stewart Easton, *Man and the World in the Light of Anthroposophy*, New York: Anthroposophic Press, 1975, p.34.

36. Steiner, *Occult Science*, p.210.

37. Rudolf Steiner addresses this theme of patterns in history in the series of lectures entitled *Egyptian Myths and Mysteries*.

38. Robert Graves, *The Greek Myths: 2*, Penguin Books, 1960, p.131.

39. Diner, p.105.

40. June Singer, *Androgyny: Toward a New Theory of Sexuality*, Garden City: Anchor Books, 1977, pp. 64 – 65.

41. Graves, Vol. 1, p.339.

42. Rudolf Steiner, *World History in the Light of Anthroposophy*, London: Rudolf Steiner Press, 1977, p.80.

43. Ibid.

44. Ibid., p.84.

45. Edouard Schuré, *The Great Initiates*, New York: Steinerbooks 1976, p.269.

46. Ibid., p.390.

47. Steiner, *World History*, p.86.

48. Graves, Vol. 2, p.70.

49. Steiner, *Egyptian Myths and Mysteries*, p.102.

50. Ibid., pp.102 – 103.

51. Rudolf Steiner, *The Gospel of St John*, Spring Valley: The Anthroposophic Press Inc., 1973, p.148.

52. Steiner, *Egyptian Myths and Mysteries*, p.139.

53. Rudolf Steiner, *The Gospel of St John in Relation to the other Gospels*, London: Percy Lund Humphries and Co. Ltd., 1933, p.213.

54. Rudolf Steiner, *Ancient Myths*, Toronto: Steiner Book Centre, 1971, p.23.

55. Steiner, *The Theosophy of the Rosicrucians*, p.17.

56. Steiner, "Freimaurerei...", p.239.

57. Rudolf Steiner, *The Philosophy of Freedom*, London: Rudolf Steiner Press, 1964, pp.204 – 205.

58. Rudolf Steiner, *Results of Spiritual Investigation*, New York: Multi-Media Publishing Corp., 1973, p.112.

The Alchemy of Relationships

Betty Staley

Eldorado

Gaily bedight,
A gallant knight,
In sunshine and in shadow,
Had journeyed long,
Singing a song,
In search of Eldorado.

Life Search

Each of us in our life on earth searches for a companion or companions with whom to share the journey. The object of this quest often lives in the ideal world and beckons us in spite of heartbreak and pathos. It becomes for us an Eldorado towards which we progress. What is it in this ideal relationship that is worth all the tribulations of the search? What is it that speaks to us, calling?

When we do find the person, we see his ideal being and we hope he will see us in our best light also. It is the merging of the two that is the ideal of the quest. (Fairytales state, they married and lived happily ever after.) This search has preoccupied humanity since earliest times regardless of geography or economic strata of society, and it takes only a cursory study of literature to affirm this. The popular tune tinkles, 'Love makes the world go round', and to some extent we feel the truth of this, particularly when we extend the object of love beyond one's mate to child, parent and friend.

In the highest sense of the experience we can ask ourselves, "When I partake of this experience of love do I do so as man or woman or am I lifted beyond myself to a sense of eternal being?" The spiritual individuality that is experienced in this relationship exists on another level of human existence. But it is a reality. Because it is so difficult to achieve, it is the object of the great mythological quests such as in the Grail legend or the Arthurian tales.

When modern persons set forth on this path of exploration two signposts guide their way. One is love and the other is growth. There is an inner flagellation today to keep growing, not to remain stagnant. Changing and transcending are modern models. This growth can emerge gradually from the courage of acceptance, from the honest perspective of living the human condition, from the tender understanding of others in their striving to grow as well.

Our present society is engaged in conflict around these two signposts. Love used to have a meaning that was clear to all – love of family, God, home; the modern person re-evaluates all previously unquestioned assumptions of life.

In addition, the barraging from the media confuses us so that we think we understand love but then something new hits us and we have to rethink it again. It reminds me of the carousel with riders reaching for the brass ring. As soon as they reach and grab one, the ring loses its substance, disappears into thin air, and the rider falls off the circling base. We have lost our certainty in many ways today as we seek new answers.

The popular definition of the fulfilled life usually means having everything one wants, an exciting life, meeting many interesting people, being fancy free, having lovely surroundings, long weekends. This is the promise put to us by contemporary images and it is very difficult to resist the allure of that promise. One has to keep reminding oneself that the image is not reality. Reality could never measure up to the illusion in some ways, yet real life is so much richer and deeper, and we know it is true.

What is this signpost engraved with Love, this ideal of community, of sacrifice, this beckoner to us through all time and all being? In this chapter I will try to explore the concept of love as it is connected to relationships. Then there is the other signpost with that quizzical word Growth; changing, becoming. What is its secret meaning? The word growth has become a common cliche since the First World War. Franklin Baumer, Yale Professor, states "Becoming, it should be made clear, does not refer here merely to new and changing answers to perennial questions, which may be taken for granted, or even to great revolutions in ideas. It refers instead to a mode of thinking that contemplates everything, nature, man, society, history, God himself. . . as not merely changing, but as forever evolving into something new and different. It disbelieves in all fixities, absolutes and 'eternal' ideas. Historically speaking, its essence, as John Dewey observed apropos the impact of Darwinism on philosophy, consisted in a remarkable 'transfer of interest from the permanent to the changing.'"[1]

We are entering a new age, an age in which thousands of people are experiencing life within a deeply spiritual framework, but outside of a religious structure. This shakes the old established authorities and it sometimes makes it hard to find one's way through the myriad of spiritual disciplines and growth enhancers. The variety of groups available today to aid in growth is staggering. It is no longer embarrassing to admit that one is searching for one's true self and for the real meaning of love. The need is real and the human soul is on a definite quest. The knight of old has been transformed with inner armour and sword as he ventures out into unknown lands of spirit. This search is not casual, it sometimes means breaking up relationships as new values are being tested. At best it causes anxiety and soul trembling as the secure foundations of life are shaken. Probably one of the basic questions underlying many of today's problems is Can I grow in the way I feel I need to in the confines of a committed relationship? What is the value of commitment?

Another dominant element in this situation is a strong undercurrent of materialism, a sense that each of us must experience everything in this lifetime or we won't have the chance again. We must have a variety of mates, jobs, experiences to be truly fulfilled. Thus the search for growth becomes frenetic, often marring the legitimate needs of the modern person.

The fragility of relationships in the wake of this attack particularly takes its toll on marriage. How much can marriage bend to allow room for search, investigation, therapy, encounter, self understanding? What about dedication, devotion, communication along the way? Is there a trend where people experience the shattering only to find their true appreciation for the other, sometimes too late?

One thing is sure, this shattering knows no boundaries in class, race or religion. It is there in deeply religious families of various beliefs, as well as in close couples whose friendships with each other were deep and binding who suddenly find themselves unable to communicate, it is there with older people in their 50s, young people in their 20s. There is a singular lack of prophecy involved except that it seems if couples with a solid foundation in their relationship can be patient, there is a possibility of reconciliation, and more than that, productive growth in themselves and as a couple.

The word relationship means involvement, association, or connection. Our lives are filled with such interactions from the most superficial contact with a merchant to the deeply personal relationship we have with ourselves. In between are the hundreds of associations we have with other human beings in our living environment. "One pays a lot, we all pay a lot, for awareness. When I develop that sense of awareness, I develop by extension, a sense concerning you that does not dictate why my relationship is with you. I may have to fight you as soon as I am aware of you, I must relate to you. I must take you in. This is engagement. It is a prerequisite to any kind of love and it is difficult and necessary"[2].

When we look back at our own or another's biography, relationships stand out as the turning points and influences on the life itself. There is mystery in relationships, and something more than simple coincidence at work. From the time we are born we are involved in a deep relationship with parents and siblings. Here, we can question the origin of these relationships. Did they just happen, or is there a background to them? As we go to school, we have friends; some are stronger friendships than others, some are willful, involving anger and then 'making up', others are more casual. We find our bond with our parents changing during these school years. Then as we move into puberty, we develop new relationships, hesitant shy ones with boys, deep ties with girlfriends, long intimate conversations with an older person, a new found respect for teachers, a 'crush' on an unattainable hero. Meanwhile our relationship to parents goes through strain and stress. As we reach adulthood our relationships tend to stabilize and fall into several areas – family, friends, profession, self.

Relationships exist on two planes; one being on the horizontal plane in the areas stated above. On the vertical plane relationships exist in time and undergo metamorphosis. Some are present only for a period of time, perhaps a close childhood friendship that seems to resolve itself and be finished as we grow older. Others are active in early life and again in the older years. Some relationships carry on through many, many years undergoing cycles of change and growth.

The question of whom we meet in our relationships is one of the great mysteries of human life. It has to do with who we are, our own sense of well being, our likes and dislikes, and the events and experiences in which we find ourselves involved. How did I take the steps that led me here? If I hadn't enrolled in that class would I never have met you? How did it happen that we ever met at all? There is great wonder in these questions. And great wisdom. Sometimes we get the feeling of guidance from the spiritual world leading us just to the moment when we meet someone. We cannot imagine life without that person.

In his 8 volumes on Karmic Relationships, Rudolf Steiner explores the laws of karma and destiny that express themselves in human life. For anyone interested in such questions these books are of the greatest value. He shows here that these relationships are not chance meetings but are deeply connected to our past lives, he characterizes the different kinds of meetings we have with people – the ones where we feel immediate familiarity, sometimes great sympathy, other times great antipathy – how we dream about these people. We connect with them out of our will. Other people we meet are very interesting to us, but the interest remains on the more intellectual or aesthetic level. We seldom dream about them. He speaks of how our destiny brings us to the meeting point; it comes out of necessity. What we do from that moment on, how we relate, comes out of our own freedom. The complexity that lies behind human relationships can barely be touched upon here, but it is important to acknowledge the network of events that leads two people together. The character of the relationship can also be affected by deeds of the past. Almost always the strong attractions described above come out of past relationships, sometimes we need to compensate for wrongdoings we have committed, and we are grateful for the opportunity. Other times we have worked very positively together and we joyously pick that up again. Just pondering these suggestions can lead one to a new understanding of relationships. If we begin to think in this kind of way we find gradually that we develop an intuition about such meetings.

Our present context will be the exploration of women's relationships – friendship, long term romantic involvement, and marriage. Many of the points I will develop can be understood in other realms as well, and mainly these observations will pertain to any human being in her soul development. We have left the main path for a while to consider the question of karma. Let us now return to our signposts, Love and Growth. Rollo May defines love as the delight in the presence of the other person and an affirming of his value and development as much as one's own.[3] This seems at first like a very simple statement, but when we begin to consider the phrase "as one's own" then it appears to be quite a different story. We begin to see that Rollo May is talking about priorities, commitment, and true consideration.

Words are easy, actions are more difficult, particularly if we are to sustain them day after day. So this sentence, this definition, is a kind of mystery. There is much more behind it than it seems at first. The question of whether we can ever really define love at all is a valid one to raise. Rudolf Steiner cautions us not to feel we can express love through definition but perhaps rather through spiritual imagery.

"Suppose a man has a loving heart, and out of his loving heart he performs a loving action to another who needs love. He gives something to that other person; but he does not on that account become emptier when he performs loving actions to another; he received more, he becomes fuller, he has still more, and if he performs the loving action a second time he will again receive more. One does not become poor, nor empty, by giving love or doing loving actions, on the contrary, one becomes richer, one becomes fuller. One pours forth something into the other person, something which makes one fuller oneself. . . Love is so complex a thing that no man should have the arrogance to define it, to fathom the nature of love. Love is a symbol, a simple symbol – a glass of water, which when it is poured out becomes even fuller, gives us one quality of the workings of love".[4]

Love described in this way has a rather alchemical flavour. What really happens to the person who is loving; is it in self-surrender that one experiences oneself in another being or does one bring the other person's being into one's own soul? This sounds similar to the Greek definition of empathy – to feel into, which is a much deeper experience than sympathy – to feel with. It was empathy that was called for in Greek tragedy. It was taught that if one experienced true empathy with the characters in the play then one would experience catharsis – a cleansing and transformation. There is something of this transformative quality in love. A great deal is required to bring this about. For one thing, one has to reduce one's own feelings of self and feel within oneself the sorrows and joys of the other being. In this empathy love springs out of the soul forces and egotism is overcome. One of the magical aspects of living love in this way is that it does help develop maturity. If we were to wait until we were mature in our own right before we experienced the other person in our soul, we might never participate in such a basically human experience. So we know from the start that we are going to make mistakes and this evokes humility in confronting ourselves and our partners.

There is in our time a preoccupation with the self – the desire to develop oneself and then later to love. When taken too far it becomes egotistical. When we love another human being spiritual truths are expressed on an earthly plane. The relationship becomes a field for development. Where there is true comradeship we can feel a stirring in our soul life. For a person who seriously strives on the spiritual path it is important to love fellow human beings. In his book *Towards the 21st Century*, Dr. Lievegoed addresses this question. "In the school of love, man had to learn the first steps. Sexual love, which as such is Luciferic, is a first step in this school."[5] He outlines the four steps in the transformation of love from the personal to the love that heals the earth:

1. Sexual love between man and woman (the impulse of love was set in the astral body by Lucifer when the sexes were separated).

2. Love between parents and children – family love, inspired by Gabriel.
3. Love of the ego of another person – regardless of sex, inspired by Michael.
4. Love of mankind – inspired by Christ.

Lievegoed characterizes these four stages, showing how each one can lead to the next.[6] Mankind as a whole is working on the third stage. What does it mean to love the ego of another person, to relate to the highest aspect of that person from our highest aspect? This is a redeemed love, freely given. In transforming the personal sexual forces in love for the spiritual ego of the other person the human being is setting out on the major task of this period of evolution. Love and Growth are intimately intertwined. If one is working on a spiritual path, true love and real kindness of the heart (compassion) are experiences of the soul which strengthen the forces of consciousness. These attitudes are basic preparation for supersensible experiences. This is the task of our time. Perhaps the outrageous sanguinity of wanting to love many people in one's lifetime is an inkling of the inner reflection of this task of loving mankind. Only it is materialized, physicalized into having sexual relations with many people.

The whole ideal of love has been drawn down and often trapped in the physical. We see this acting so dangerously on the teen culture, but few of us escape regardless of age. There is the fear that if we lose the physical, what will replace it? Deeper capacities in the human soul are not given their due yet. So much emphasis is placed on the physical that it is totally out of perspective. A new understanding of love and its meaning would radically change the emphasis that is presently felt and the damage that is being done in the soul of mankind.

In Solzhenitzen's Harvard Address, June 1978, he called attention to two aspects which he called the psychic disease of the 20th century – hastiness and superficiality. If we begin to see how prevalent these attitudes are we can then trace their influence on relationships, whether they be friendships or marriage, and definitely we can see their effects on the parent-child relationship.

We have been discussing these attitudes in this chapter. Solzhenitzen feels so strongly about them he called these symptoms the Decline of the West. The hastiness and superficiality have affected women as well as men. In the haste of being 'equal with men' women have taken on men's roles without adapting them to their true nature. There is much to do to awaken society to the gifts that both men and women bring to culture, and to evaluate these gifts. Earlier I spoke of a new attitude which does seek to reach the ego of the other person. Because women have often put priority on relationship this quality can offer help for this new age. But women and men are both vulnerable to the superficiality of our time. So often the new freedoms and the search for an independent identity sucks them into the trap of thinking that freedom must express itself in sexuality. The true awakening is often missed. In my conversations with teenagers I have found that they understand that one can have love without sexuality, and that sexuality without love is crude. They are uncomfortable with it. The coarse posters and movies would not lead us to this conclusion, but the young people are being drowned in this vortex of materialism, often against everything they truly believe.

One of the major aspects of growth in regard to love is the unfolding of certain attitudes over the long run. We have to learn to face ourselves. We do not do this in casual or quick relationships. But we can learn to develop patience and learn to face the shadow side of ourselves (the lower self or the double as it is sometimes called) as it shows itself in these kinds of relationships. In this way love and growth enhance each other.

The struggle to understand the higher nature of love and of growth involves grappling with the nuance of the word 'transformation'. Our wooden signposts of love and growth standing on two diverting paths would be transformed into vines. The wooden posts instead of being hard and angular would acquire life and become green and blossoming. The two vines of love and growth would intertwine, and poetically speaking, if they grew in a healthy manner, would give birth to the grape of the new wine. This transformation would transcend the onesidedness of either vine – love overly expresed without growth becomes enmeshed in self-sacrifice or martyrdom, sentimentality; growth without regard to love becomes egotism. Transcended they become the offering of a new consciousness, the fruit of labour and commitment.

Friendships provide a stage for the acting out of human drama and the cultivation of love. Although the degree of intensity varies with each relationship the room for growth is always there. Friendships can come and go, but a deep friendship invested with emotional involvement carries the possibility of pain as well as joy.

Women have always sought friendship, often they have centred around household tasks such as washing clothes or caring for the children. Such relationships have provided support, an outlet for expressions of frustration, and companionship during otherwise dull times. These relationships, however, have always taken second place to the marriage. In more recent times women's friendships have become more openly acknowledged. Their value has been seen in their own right, demanding time and emotional involvement. Of course, friendships for single women take on a more important rôle, providing the companionship and support that is shared by a husband.

Women are giving each other strong support today in developing new aspects of their personalities. They are exploring what they are giving and receiving in their male-female relationships and raising questions of commitment.

Women are finding that much of what they had demanded in the past of their husbands can indeed be met through a woman to woman relationship. In some ways this is removing a strain from a husband's having to fulfill every need. The more a woman feels the strength of relationships the freer she is to relate to her husband without undue dependence.

Friendships also go through cycles of development similar to marriage. As one gets into the forties the value of friendship increases and becomes more and more critical. As a person ages she accepts the friends she has without judgment.

Woman-man friendships are another question altogether. It is a contention by some that there can never be a true platonic relationship between a man and woman because of the potential for projection of the animus and anima. Others find the satisfaction of a man-woman friendship to be of great value. The acceptance of such a relationship relates to the maturity of the primary (marriage) relationship. Such a relationship is of great value because each friend can benefit from the point of view of the opposite sex.

Earlier in this book the evolution of masculine and feminine was discussed. The characteristics of male and female were examined in their ancient and modern manifestations. What is left for us to do now is to examine woman and man in relationship. Here we are confronted by one of the greatest mysteries of life, and I would not presume to have any secret answers. To come back to this subject I would like to place before you several images coming out of mythology which stand as archetypal pictures of man and woman in relationship, and then examine them in relation to contemporary needs and understanding.

When we say today that we are entering a new age we are referring to a new kind of consciousness that considers both the masculine and feminine approaches to life as equally valid. It also considers that each human being, whether male or female, is seeking balance of masculine and feminine forces within one's own nature. This is not to eradicate the character of each sex but to bring more consciousness of one's own sex and of the desire to develop the ego.

It was described earlier how in the beginnings of culture matriarchy tended to rule society. Here the senses were stressed, woman was less incarnated into her body and more attuned to the spiritual. The intuitive side of life ruled. After what many cultures described as the flood the one-sided approach of the subconscious was annihilated because it had become decadent. Balance was needed and a new form of society emerged with the masculine element more dominant.

In the overthrow of the matriarchy and take-over by patriarchy the will was emphasised rather than the senses. Discipline, learning, reason and logic were highly valued. Group control became stronger than the individual. But today we are aware that this one-sidedness has become decadent too. This kind of thinking has given us mastery over the earth and brought great achievements, but it has gone too far. A new approach is needed. Some of us sense that crisis is at hand, and instead of flood we may end in fire this time.

In the Tarot cards the woman is seen as the water process, and water is the subconscious mind. Water which does not hold form of itself but fills the form of the vessel, water in its misty density sometimes blurring the clarity of the sun. But too much unconsciousness leads to lack of control.

The male is seen as the fire process. We can look back to Prometheus as the bringer of fire as an image of this change from matriarchy to patriarchy, and we can also see the freedom that was given to human kind when the human soul was released from the control of the subconscious. But too much consciousness, too defined tight rigid boundaries lead to rigidity. The harmonizing of the two consciousnesses calls for the development of thinking and feelings in a way that they merge and enrich each other.

In the Irish legend *The Crock of Gold*, by James Stephens, a strong image is presented. The Tree of Knowledge becomes too strong and encloses Caitilin in Murrachu from the Tree of Life. The wall, it is predicted, will not be toppled until Thought and Instinct are wed. The god Angus Og appears to her and asks her "What is the greatest thing in the world?" He tells her it is "Divine Imagination". She says, "Happiness is the greatest thing in the world". Her father has said, "Common sense is the greatest thing in the world". Angus Og reveals that the Divine Imagination may only be known through the thoughts of his creatures. "A man has said, 'Common sense' and a woman has said 'Happiness' are the greatest things in the world. These things are male and female for Common sense is Thought and Happiness is Emotion, and until they embrace in Love the will of Immensity cannot be fruitful."[7]

The god goes on to describe that humanity has never had a true marriage of these, that each has really been mating with an idea of the other, rather than the reality. "Man is Thought and Woman is Intuition, and they have never mated. There is a gulf between them and it is called Fear, and what they fear is that their strengths shall be taken from them and they may no longer be tyrants. Wisdom is the son of Thought and Intuition and his names are also Innocence and Adoration and Happiness."[8]

This made me think about a question often asked by women in groups, "Why is there such polar opposition between husband and wife? If I say black, he says white, and I do the same. It is as if we were at war." The competition that is sensed often comes out in conversations and can be quite uncomfortable for a third person. Is there something in this image of fear?

To get back to the story, the god Angus Og calls out:

" . . . . . the world has forgotten me. In all my nation there is no remembrance of me. I, wandering on the hills of my country, am lonely indeed. I am the desolate god forbidden to utter my happy laughter. I hide the silver of my speech and the gold of my merriment. I live in the holes of the rocks and the dark caves of the sea. Where I have kissed a bird has flown; where I have trod a flower has sprung. But Thought has snared my birds in his nests and sold them in the marketplaces. Who will deliver me from Thought, from the base holiness of Intellect, the maker of chains and traps? Who will save me from the holy impurity of Emotion, whose daughters are Envy, Jealousy and Hatred, who plucks from flowers to ornament her lusts and my little leaves to shrivel on the breasts of infamy? Lo, I am sealed in the caves of nonentity until the head and the heart shall come together in fruitfulness, until Thought has wept for Love, and Emotion has purified herself to meet her lover."[9]

He then goes on to prophecy his own imprisonment until the time when the head of a woman and the heart of a man are filled with the Divine Imagination. In this image is the task that lies ahead, the bringing of balance to each, so that whole man and woman may merge with each other in peace and consciousness, a holy union.

Jung contends that mythology is an accounting of ancient experiences occurring far back in the forming of the human race. Yet, these experiences echo into the modern time and have formed basic attitudes prevailing today. Although we try to rectify them we are contending with something more powerful than is outwardly obvious.

In a 9th grade mythology course we examined the influence of myths. We studied the myth of Adam and Eve and then examined a related one entitled Adam, Lilith and Eva. In the latter account Lilith was created at the same time as Adam and out of the same material. But because of her magic powers and vanity she disappeared and Eva was then created out of Adam's rib. The students were fascinated with this image and eagerly discussed the different attitude they would have had if they had been brought up on this version rather than on Adam and Eve with the negative picture of Eve tempting innocent Adam with the apple.

Several months after this experience I came upon a fascinating book entitled *Israeli Women, the Reality behind the Myths* by Lesley Hazelton.[10] Hazelton examines this myth in relation to the way women have been regarded in Judaism and goes further to describe the effect of different myths, often contradictory, on the Israeli woman today.

Inasmuch as the myth of Adam and Eve has become part of the Western world's religious and literary heritage the power of this myth is of the greatest magnitude. In Hazelton's account of the myth (Colum's is much more vague[11]) Eva refuses male domination, she dares the forbidden by uttering the magic name of God, and disappears. The image of Lilith with her supernatural powers becomes rejected and she is pushed into the role of temptress, the seducer. In comparison Eva, who is also shown as a temptress, is mild. She is responsible for seducing Adam, but then has to be his helpmate when they are driven out of Paradise. She feels pain in bearing children from that time on. The subjection of Lilith to her position as evil may also reflect the domination of male society in the overthrow of feminine control.

"In her flight from Adam, Lilith found refuge by the shores of the Red Sea, a region abounding in lascivious demons, to whom she bore children at the rate of more than a hundred a day."[12] But lest the demographic balance between demons and humans became too lopsided, God's specific punishment was that one hundred of her demon children should perish each day. In bitter revenge, Lilith therefore preys on human children, especially on newborn male infants, who are particularly vulnerable to her until the time of their circumcision, eight days after birth. Unless protected by magic amulets with inscriptions such as 'Lilith out, Adam and Eve in' and horrifying drawings of Lilith as a scrawny hag, used until recently by Oriental Jews, the infant is in mortal danger. In the Zohar, one of the main cabbalistic books, Lilith reaches the pinnacle of evil by becoming the consort of Satan, the epitome of wickedness and the forces of darkness . . . absolved of all blame for his inability to co-exist with Lilith, the witch, Adam was now free to establish his dominance over a much lesser creation – Eve.[13]

Woman is put into an ambivalent position here, she is relegated to a sexual object; at the same time she is shameful and evokes fear in the male. From Robert Graves and Raphael Patai's book *Hebrew Myths, the Book of Genesis* (McGraw-Hill 1966) Hazelton related more of the Lilith myth. This includes God's creation of Eve One whom he creates out of bones, tissues, muscles, blood, glandular secretions, skin, and hair. Adam was repelled by her and God causes her to vanish. Now God tries again. He creates Eve Two who is adorned with superficial beauty. Now Adam does not see her sensuality but indulges in romanticism. Hazelton asks a very basic question:

"Who is this Eve? The weak-willed, mindlessly evil temptress and seductress of Adam, bringing about his degradation and downfall and her own into the bargain? Or a courageous seeker of knowledge and truth, reaching out for the symbolic fruit as for experience and adventure? She might well have been seeking an escape from her limitations and a resurrection of the first Eve, the reality of her own body and experience as opposed to the superficiality of the second Eve, real only as seen in Adam's eyes. Could she have been yearning for the grandeur and independence of Lilith? We are never given a chance to find out, for Eve's very existence is merely a vehicle for introducing shame, guilt, and the toil of labour into society, with no blame attached to man. The woman took the Fall, for she was set up for it from the start. And with that Fall, eroticism is conquered by guilt, and woman's sexuality is reduced to a male appendage."[14]

Before the time of Christ, women were seen as leading men into temptation with womanly wiles and manipulation – the teasing veil, the beckoning eyes, the imprisoning embrace which man must learn to withstand. During that time the male was seeking to ground human life on the earth, to master its forces, conquer it, tame it, and exploit it for human life.

Since the time of Christ, women have become the symbol of purity (another exaggerated image which lives on in its ambivalent polarity). Here she is a power which softens the hardening forces of male strength. Eva the tempter of Adam has become Ave (the Virgin Mary), an image of worship and reverence.

Rudolf Steiner describes the Fall of Man as having been instigated by Lucifer who works through the astral body of the human being – in the sexual desire, to bring man out of the state of Paradise. Separated from this union with the spirit mankind could be free. Mankind owes its freedom to this act of Eve and Adam.

Women today in the Western world bear a conflict between these polarities in their beings and men relate to them ambivalently as well. Woman as temptress – woman as virgin. In the *Hazards of Being Male*, Herb Goldberg describes this double conflict the man feels.[15] The problem is there and forms part of the mystery of man and woman.

Part of the complexity is that man and woman relate on various levels. On the biological level men and women complement each other and need each other to carry on the species. The soul life, which is influenced by both the biological and spiritual elements, gives rise to a difference in the psychological experiences of male and female. Both souls have different longings, impulses, needs, and questions. When a person is completely one sided and acts too feminine or too masculine he or she comes across as being rather childish and silly. It is hard for others to take the person seriously as an individual rather than strictly as a man or woman. In our everyday life the woman seems to be more harmed by this stereotyping because society has fixed the woman's role over the ages, whereas the man has been allowed to develop more of his individual capacities. It is women who had their feet bound, or were forced into tight waist cinches. Women have been evaluated as to whether they can advance in a particular profession in spite of being women. It is generally known that human beings tend to live up to the expectations that are held of them. So it is not surprising that women have attained leadership in certain areas only! "To all who fear an upheaval of our social structure through accepting women as individuals and not as females, we must reply that a social structure in which the status of one-half of humanity is unworthy of a human being is itself in great need of improvement."[16]

The level of spiritual equality between women and men is in the Ego. Both are human and as such have an individuality which increasingly determines development during life.

In this chapter we have been examining the various factors of a relationship – the question of love and growth, the male and female characteristics that enter into relationships. The whole question of the nature of male-female relationships is a complex one. In the following pages we will focus on marriage (or partnership) as a main area of concentration.

Metamorphosis and Transcendence

Each one of us has a unique history. We pass through phases of life from childhood to adulthood gaining new capacities and losing old ones. We feel the changes occurring but are not always conscious of what they are or what they mean. It is only on reflection that we can survey the past – the paths leading to crucial turning points, the meetings with special people, the critical decisions made. In each phase of life there are laws working, just as there are laws working in nature.

Seeds of one cycle take root in the next cycle and blossom in the succeeding one. As we work to understand these laws, perspective develops and we come to regard life as an organic unfolding of individuality. With this comes a deeper appreciation for the richness of life in each of its stages. We come to understand growth and transformation, and hopefully we develop perception so we can make the needed changes.

Just as each individual passes through cycles, so does a relationship. During each stage we experience particular needs and solutions. In each relationship there are three basic elements. First there is the individuality of each person including the past and present of that person's life. Second, there is the phase of life the individual is in. Third, because relationships go through stages, it is important to consider what stage a relationship is in. For example, if a relationship begins in a couple's forties, the early phase will represent the quality of the twenties and then move quickly through the phases until it comes to the period of life the couple is in. In addition to these three aspects, there are such influences as the environment, the culture, and the period of history.

It is not easy to generalize about relationships and we need to keep this in mind. These are not recipes but suggestions. Even so, it is important to bear in mind that when we ourselves experience crisis (usually towards the end of one phase) the theories tend to go out the window and we are most aware of our own pain. We are confronted with ourselves face to face. Everything of supportive help is needed to get through this period and into the next phase (when the feeling finally does occur one morning, "Ah, how wonderful, a new day has dawned!"). Once into the new phase it is helpful to look back and find that the warning signs were all there pointing to the impending crisis, but we may have chosen to ignore them.

It is my hope that the reader will not find this too theoretical, but helpful in their own life growth and in the growth of their friends, partner, children, and parents. All of us as human beings share the reality of confrontation with change.

Dreamers of Dreams - The Twenties

> We are the music makers,
> And we are the dreamers of dreams,
> Wandering by lone sea-breakers,
> And sitting by desolate streams;
> World-losers and world-forsakers,
> On whom the pale moon gleams;
> Yet we are the movers and shakers
> Of the world forever,
> It seems.

I remember canning peaches in my mid-twenties. It was a late summer's day and I started thinking about life, careers, and contributions. I was a young wife and mother and at my feet my first born child was crawling. It was long before I knew of life-cycles, but it came to me then that these were my 'at-home' years. As I thought about the future I saw the thirties as the transitional years, perhaps I would work part-time, and the forties as my professional years. There was a very settling quality to these thoughts and I felt at peace with them.

Looking back now, in my late forties with twenty years of teaching behind me, I can only smile at the satisfaction with which I had laid out my goals. Even though life has taken a different course there is still the essence of truth in that plan; each period has had a different emphasis even though the full-time years at home did not last as long as expected.

The twenties are a time of adventure and stability, a time of paradox; two needs and two goals often trying to occupy the same space. A time of dreamers of dreams. We know it all, we have all the answers, all the hopes and all the confidence. I remember a young friend of about 25 years of age saying to me, "Those things won't happen to us because we know all about them". I smiled and inwardly mumbled, "Just wait". Three years later his perspective was quite different. He said, "I feel as if I'm coming from a different place. The same things don't satisfy me."

Couples who marry in their twenties, particularly in the early twenties, frequently lack varied experience. On the surface they have been brought together by strong emotional attraction and together they dream of building their future. They relish their similarities and focus on what they enjoy doing together. They lay out their plans much as I laid out my 'at-home' years. What happens?

Life begins to meet them and challenges their certainty. Things don't work out as promised, there are unknown byways. Their arrogance is challenged and the realities begin asserting themselves.

The particular stresses of the early years are different for the wife and for the husband. The honeymoon period ends and there are conflicts over parents-in-law, jealousies, disagreements over places to live or means of livelihood. The period of disenchantment slowly settles in. The wife is adjusting to a different focus. When the couple was courting she was being catered to; very often she was the centre of attention, and her young man would think of exciting things to do or presents to surprise her with. Once married, the young wife finds herself more often catering to her husband. Gradually, she realises that she has built up an image of her husband as the great protector, the strong man. She begins to see chinks in his armour, feel some doubts. Sometimes she ignores these, other times she is confused and feels guilty about having them.

There is an expression used by Congreve in *The Way of the World* which describes her change of status. She is "dwindling into a wife".[17] This change of status affects her self-image and confidence, and much of her personality has to reshape to conform to her husband's wishes, needs and demands. More often than not it is the wife undergoing this change, and the inner stress resulting is one of the many drains on a young wife's psyche.

Even the most sophisticated young woman still finds herself trying to fulfil the man's expectation of her. Every woman in love unconsciously adapts herself to what she thinks he wants her to be. This is not done without some ambivalence. Whether she admits to it or not most assertive women go through this to some degree. She will be soft and pliant, sensitive to the man's moods and responsive to his wishes, expressed or implied. However, once she is secure she may allow the more assertive side to emerge, and this may then create a disruption in her husband's sense of well-being. He feels the loss and does not know how to explain it. Something is gone.

One of the most heartrending adjustments wives, particularly those at home, make is in the pattern of emotional expression between themselves and their husbands. As his job becomes more and more consuming the original warmth subsides and there is a let-down in the emotional experience.

Another aspect is that as the married woman becomes mother she assumes an almost sexless role. Philip Slater states, "It is only young unmarried girls who are allowed to be entirely female . . . As soon as they are married they are expected to mute their sexuality somewhat, and when they become mothers their neutralization is carried even further".[18]

Wendell Berry in *The Unsettling of America* points out a very important historical change affecting the place of wife in society. He shows that the *difference of work* (italics mine) done by husband and wife within the context of wholeness has become separated to a *division of work*. "The first sexual division comes about when nurture is made the exclusive concern of women."[19] He sees that this separation of roles signified that neither nurture nor womanhood was very important. (I might add that this is a great loss to manhood when seen from a modern perspective.) Woman is further isolated into becoming a purchasing agent for the family. Separated from her husband's work, her children's lives, she was relegated to the position of chauffeur and marketer; she was a natural victim of advertisers warning her to be a fresh attractive magnet for her husband. Her fears and doubts were expressed publicly and capitalized on. This gulf became a problem for husband and wife. The sharing of life in the household was no longer nourishing a true centre of their life together. Mutual dependence gave rise to two distinct functions, one of which was valued more highly. The husband came home after he finished his work, but many husbands do not consider home a place to 'feel at home' in, but prefer their offices or neighbourhood hangouts. The woman is isolated causing her to be seen in an unrealistic way. She swims in sexual romance, bathes in sentimentality which reaches her through popular songs and stories, making her believe that love and physical beauty go hand in hand, that love is related to young people "even though", as Berry says, "love is said to last forever",[20] that marriage is the end-all of life, and that love makes everything all right.

The young wife is at home centering her life around the needs of her husband and child. She is there to help carry out their dream. She takes care of the house, tends the children when ill, gets the car and appliances fixed, supervises house repairs, shops, straightens out the bank account, has an ear for people's problems, makes dinner or organises the weekend, and is ready for her husband when he returns home.

There is little she can point to with genuine accomplishment although she is the centre of activities. Her tasks are renewable, the clothes get washed, dirtied, washed again, so too the dishes and floor. In comparison with her husband's work hers can seem demeaning. If his job is not entirely meaningful at least he has a paycheck at the end of the week or the chance of promotion. She faces the same routine day in and day out. Even for a woman who thoroughly enjoys housework her relation to her husband undergoes a change that should be looked at.

Even when women take jobs, they don't often commit themselves to these but see them as temporary. Their first commitment is the family. Other women see their main job as loving a man and being loved by him, not to complicate this task in any way. So, even though she may be out in the world she does not place priority on her job, and thus she does not gain the same satisfaction from her work as her husband does. When a person cannot take her job seriously, it is hard for her to take herself seriously.

For the woman at home (and in many cases, women at jobs too) the world becomes very isolated into a small self-contained unit, especially for women who were active in community or college, and used to being in a group. This is especially true of a young career woman who marries and then stays at home. Now she is confined to a smaller circle of movement and becomes dependent on her husband for her main source of stimulation. Her needs then concentrate on the children who cannot fulfil them; it is an unfair unconscious demand. This isolation causes brooding which intensifies the isolation and leads to alienation. Depression is one of the major women's illnesses, particularly for housewives. The result is often erratic judgment.

Jessie Barnard has gone to lengths to carefully document the mental and emotional state of the health of wives and the possible reasons for it in order to place the evidence "beyond cavil or frivolous disparagement or ridicule".[21] The housewife syndrome is not given seriousness and yet it is driving many women insane. To ask a healthy personality to fit herself into such a pattern is to drive a woman crazy. What may have satisfied women in previous times is not doing so today. Perhaps they had no choice previously or perhaps the isolation now is of a different character and more poignant. This is not to suggest that women should not spend time at home, but it is to raise questions about how people live in communities, what is expected of each partner, and most of all to let the women know that these emotionally stressed feelings are normal and need to be addressed.

Anne Morrow Lindberg pondered the strain on the young housewife, and her creative talent poured forth the *Gift from the Sea*. From her personal experience she writes, "Here is a strange paradox. Woman instinctively wants to give, yet resents giving herself in small pieces. Basically is this a conflict? Or is it an oversimplification of a many-stranded problem? I believe that what woman resents is not so much giving herself in pieces as giving herself purposelessly. What we fear is not so much that our energy may be leaking away through small outlets as that it may be going down the drain. We do not see the results of our giving as concretely as man does in his work . . . It is hard even to think of it as purposeful activity, so much of it is automatic. Woman herself begins to feel like a telephone exchange or a laundromat."[22]

Today we can see that this question of purpose in life is not just one that is gnawing at women. Men, too, are being adversely affected by separation and purposelessness. But women still remain the prime target. "No longer fed by a feeling of indispensability or purposefulness, we are hungry, and not knowing what we are hungry for, we fill up the void with endless distractions, always at hand, unnecessary errands, compulsive duties, social niceties. And for the most part, to little purpose. Suddenly the spring is dry; the well is empty,"[23] Lindbergh continues.

As we look around us today we see many young men expressing an interest in nurturing and in the whole question of shared living, shared responsibilities of marriage. Men's involvement in birth, nutrition, and children may only be happening in a small group who are pursuing an alternative lifestyle, but it is part of the hope for the future. In the film *Kramer vs. Kramer*, we get a sense of the change that being a caring parent demands. It is difficult to make work top priority if one is a caring parent and as such responsible for a child's well being. A new appraisal of life's worth and our direct involvement in it is part of the way young people can heal the symptoms of isolation.

In spite of all the problems that marriage bears for women it is amazing to see how many still marry. There is something of the ideal in human relationships that still shines through all that is imperfect. Yet in our day it is important to bring in light rather than cast the long dark shadows. Society has brought women to see marriage as the epitome of happiness and the indoctrination has been thorough, at least for all generations up to the present. Older societies made no promises, marriage was an economic and social contract, love was the fruit of daily caring for each other. In *Fiddler on the Roof* it is Tevya's daughters and their talk of marrying that causes him to ask Golda, "Do you love me?" She answers "Do I what?" Her summation is that after 25 years of caring for him and sharing his bed and home she supposes she does.

Marriage as the solution to happiness is heavily sponsored by the commercial world of advertising and popular culture. However, there are young women, more now than ever before in the Western world who are choosing to remain single, and whether this radically changes society we will have to wait and see.

A woman bears other stresses in marriage besides the relationship with her husband. Society places its weight on her too. The outer world values strength and activity but women have been trained to be passive and dependent. The conflict of values can cause strain, and many women answer it by holding themselves back from active involvement in society. This split intensifies as a woman reaches her late twenties.

What stresses are on the man in marriage? The evidence shows that men survive longer when married, have better mental health, and choose marriage over and over again, even though they verbally condemn it.

"The discrepancy between the husband's horrendous inner picture of his marriage and its actual observable beneficent effects on him is a measure of the ineluctable conflict built into marriage. Human beings want dramatically opposite things; stability and adventure; security and variety; excitement and thrills, but also a fair haven to retreat to when the fun and games are over."[24]

Men resent marriage because it is sexually restrictive and because it demands emotional responsibilities. These areas are undergoing changes in favour of the husband's role. Even the courts recognise that the husband should not carry the full economic burden any longer.

Although men, on the whole, benefit from marriage they too suffer more subtle effects, many of which are described in *The Hazards of Being Male*. These lie in the areas of psychological dependence and ambivalence about women in the first place. We could add that they experience a split in that they are fascinated with the single unattached woman but feel suffocated by their wives (and, I should add, by their mothers). So there is an advance and retreat on the emotional level in marriage which men experience but do not always consciously take hold of. Even with this difficulty most men benefit more from marriage than women do.

With all of the strains and differences in marriage the question of whether a particular one will survive these challenges calls for the two people to understand each other and know how to respond so as to help deepen the relationship. But it has to go further. To understand what has to be done is not enough. One has to do what needs to be done. We have such a tendency today to get stuck in thinking that understanding is enough. We have to apply our wills in working through the problems, to assess them realistically, and to act in a constructive manner.

The first year of marriage is the crucial time for making these adjustments, although adaptability to stress is called for all through married life. Some successes, some failures come. The couple reach heights and depths, and each demands its own adjustments. They begin to see how aspects of the other, the perfect image begins to get shaken. Because the young person in this period is guided by emotion (by feeling)[25] judgment is subjective. Each has strong feelings. They form friendships according to emotional likes, they join in situations depending on how they feel about them. They direct themselves outwardly. Instead of asking "Who am I?" as they did in their late teens they switch to "What shall I do in life?", "How shall we shape our dreams?" and "Can I attain the impossible?".

The young couple sees its years in the twenties as a time to build a foundation for the future, to aim towards stability, even if they don't want it just yet. Action becomes the guidepost. Somewhere in the 29th-30th year most young people expect to be settled. There is some conflict during this time over how much experimentation and how much commitment should be sought. Here life style varies depending on whether the wife is working or at home.

Working women do not become so alienated since they are stimulated by being in the world. The marriages do not become empty shells. On the other hand these women wonder if they are not missing something in not having families. The working woman often shares many of the same goals as the young men except that at the end of this period she searches for the man of her dreams, or if married, decides it is time to have children. Many young single women in the working world act as men did in the last decades and try to prove themselves with quick advancement, becoming aggressive and goal orientated. By 28-30 she is frought with crisis over whether she is going to be able to change the pattern when she wants. A fear sets in that she will be only a career woman. An unconscious concern is the risk she has taken by being too successful and competitive. Has she frightened away interested suitors? Surprisingly, I have heard this concern even among women leading a looser life style than the majority.

Marriages in the late teens or twenties are not necessarily conscious relationships in the first place. There is strong emotional and physical attraction pulling the couple together. They are enthralled with how similar they are – "He likes what I like". There is a great deal of reflection or selflove taking place. The ideals of marriage are very high, even in the children of broken or destructive families. The young person never quite believes that what she sees around her could ever happen to her. Within a few years she is often repeating the environmental pattern of marriage in her own life. The hope, the promise, the momentary feeling of bliss blinds couples to the hardships that follow. I recently had a conversation with a group of young mothers, under 19 years of age, all divorced with children. They were bitter about life and about marriage. Now they felt trapped, could not go on and get training (none had finished high school), could not afford babysitting, were lonely living in apartments, couldn't leave the baby alone and could only feel despair.

It is difficult to confront young people in love with these images. How does one know it will last, or if it really is love? What will it be like when the glow wears off? There is so much we have to do to awaken ourselves to realities, to the beauty of love when it is truly so, and the responsibility of caring for that love so that it does not go sour.

The process of being in love is a stage; the partners are very involved with the process. We could say they are in love with love, or we could say they are 'ready' for it to happen. They care about being attractive to one another, see the highest in the other person. Inwardly, emotion is pulling at the young people. The ups and downs, highs and lows, only begin gradually to conflict as reality meets ideal. The inner work of maturing is often cut short by young marriages. They slip into expected roles without thinking. What is it then that reaches a height at the end of this period? The gap between reality and ideal has become almost unacceptable. Basically each person in the marriage is wanting his or her needs fulfilled. Because they live in the romantic tradition and are in love, each assumes the other can read or intuit his or her needs. Slowly and with much pain they find that it doesn't happen. They become disappointed, annoyed, lose the glow around the specialness of the other person, feel anger, and hatred – ending in the suppression of even the romantic, feeling life. This is one of the critical experiences in marriage and the most misunderstood. Each partner is confused and lonely, filled with ugly emotions and doubt.

Marriages in the twenties are based on projection. When the projection is removed, each is a stranger. By resolving the projection each is more integrated. But this process is painful. Couples are even more confused during this period because Western society is so rooted in feelings. They feel duty bound to hold onto the earlier image of marriage and romanticism or else something is very wrong. The subtlety of love has little place in advertisements which barrage the young person. Consumerism is directed at perpetuating this period.

There is an unsettling feeling that things must change and at the same time there is very little help given in society to assist this change. The man's desire for conquest must be recognised as persisting immaturity; the woman's persistence in seeing the world through romantic eyes must yield to a deeper sense of loving. Both must feel the normalcy of this change without feeling they have failed to continue the old 'high' of life. This is a critical time. It is as if the couple is being asked to remarry now that they know the responsibilities that have been accepted. If the couple can survive the first seven years of marriage there is a chance they can develop the capacity for intimacy which can only come after each has developed a sense of personal identity based on solidity.

Waking Up - 28-35

When people near the age of 28 they begin to have a feeling that it is time to get serious about life, that somehow they should have a sense of what their future looks like. The time for fooling around is nearing an end and it is time to look life squarely in the eye. There is also a feeling that the time is at hand and that innocence of life is undergoing a change. One evening when I was 32 my husband and I had discussed the fact that so far we had had a blessed life. No challenges had come along that we couldn't meet. We felt like children who had not been tested and almost felt cheated. The next day I was in an automobile accident and it was the beginning of a year of almost perpetual crisis.

A sensitive awareness of others begins to dawn, softening the arrogance of the twenties. Self-doubt enters and one gets the feeling that it is time to take responsibility, not just sit on the sidelines and criticise. "I too am vulnerable" is a sense that gradually awakens, bringing with it a poignancy of its own. This occurred so strongly in my own life. My husband and I were giving advice to a friend about how to handle marital problems. A few weeks later we were facing almost the same difficulties. We blushed at how simplistic our answers had been; we realised how unsympathetic we had been to our friend's pain.

This 7 year period is a time of great loneliness. The intellect is sharp and there is a strong feeling of separateness which often breaks a previously strong 'togetherness'. The partners begin to stand back and observe each other. What they find is not always to their liking, especially since the glamour is gone. There is a certain amount of guilt involved too; she feels guilty because he is no longer the romantic hero. Instead she becomes cool, critical, objective; his weaknesses, his faults, stand out. Each one stands more naked in front of the other. This feeling of judgment is a two-way street. The person also turns the judgment on himself and in the overwhelming experience of seeing one's own faults out of balance one often withdraws into one's own self, with the intention to concentrate on fewer things and to do them well. The person returns to the question of the late teens, "What am I?" "What am I able to achieve?" "Have I found my work in the world?" We find a pattern emerging in our times, particularly if the woman has spent the early years at home. The man begins to withdraw; the woman begins to wake up to the desire to move out into the world, to find out if the world values her.

There is a discomfort with the plans the couple made in the twenties; they don't fit anymore. The priorities have changed.

Becoming dissatisfied, each individual feels restricted, narrow, and turns this criticism outward, blaming the spouse. The sense of impending crisis causes one to question, "Is this my mate for life?"

In another way life becomes more rational, more orderly. The couple address issues more logically, make decisions such as where to settle down, whether to buy a house, what neighbourhood is right. The feeling of establishing roots is strong. I can think of many times when people this age applying for jobs have commented, "We are looking for the community in which to finally settle down. It is time to put down roots." I sometimes see a smile on my colleagues' faces as they know from experience there is no absolutely right place, it cannot be thought out logically, other forces are at work that have to do with destiny.

Whereas satisfaction tends to strengthen outwardly as one feels "Now we're on our way", the contentment with the marriage starts sliding. Additional strain is added because social life is often restricted to the family or a few close friends, encouraging a kind of boredom. Particularly conscientious parents suffer during this time because they are reluctant to leave their children for an occasional weekend. Instead they forfeit the couple relationship that needs renewing and deepening over and over again. It is of utmost importance that the couple get some time away to face each other without household chores involved, to explore a new place, to wake up in a different bedroom, to go out for breakfast. The need to renew the intimacy of marriage, to recapture the mood of early love is a strongly compelling one and so often is submerged in the busyness (or business) of life. The man is feeling very competent and now starts telling his wife to go out and do something interesting. He wants her to broaden herself, become a companion and mother rather than mostly a mother. The way she takes it usually makes her feel threatened. "I'm not good enough. How will I ever interest him?" She is already feeling impatient and narrow, and now he, too, finds her unworthy the way she is. She begins to wonder what it would be like to leave the security of her home. Her husband, when he contemplates her life at home, knows he would be bored silly and is glad not to have to live her kind of life. At the same time he likes the results of it for himself and feels caught in a trap. Because her life is so narrow she depends on him for exciting news from work, but he is not particularly interested in talking about it with her. Gail Sheehy points out in *Passages* that there is also fear working in him that if she really became preoccupied with something outside the home, she would not care for him and feed him. This contradiction between what he wants and what he fears makes him feel guilty. There is a push me, pull you or yoyo syndrome at work during this time.[26]

The wife often senses this and pulls away, stops being supportive as she becomes more and more preoccupied, frenzied, and threatened. They often miss each other just when they need each other the most. She senses that he is changing. She tries to become less dependent so that he won't feel trapped. She pulls away to help him, but it backfires. He feels she doesn't care and is disappointed, lost. One often feels nothing will work out in the right way. He wants her to become more interesting and productive. The result is a frantic pursuit of this fad or that, but she finds it difficult to stay with anything for a prolonged period of time.

I remember this feeling well. I had just turned 28 and decided I would take my Master's degree. I didn't really know why, but I felt I had to do something 'important' and also be preparing for the future. I went to the University to enroll, stood in long lines, became so frenzied with the system, that I turned around and went home. I had a strange feeling that day as I drove home. In some ways I felt I had failed, I had not faced the complexities of modern life. I had felt intimidated by something most eighteen year olds, including myself, could perfectly well handle at that age.

Not long after, I spoke to a friend who had re-entered a community college in her late thirties and found that many women shared the fear I had had on that day, to the point where some of them would not even ask where the rest rooms were. This fear of re-entry at a time when self worth is so low is a serious problem. It led me to ponder the changes I had experienced in my own life and also to re-evaluate the dynamic of marriage, particularly as it pertains to woman's role. I pictured myself as a co-ed, active, alive, vital, interested. The world was stimulating and I felt excited to be part of it. Then for two years in the working world my husband and I were companions, sharing experiences, feeling very strongly we were doing meaningful work, exploring career possibilities, alive, equal to the task. Then I pictured my feelings after I became pregnant and stopped working. Everything slowed down. I was alone much of the time, took long walks, became inward, brooding, visited my husband's grandmother in a convalescent home, made baby clothes, did some artwork, and waited. That ever present waiting for my husband to come home, wanting the previous excitement we had brought each other. After the baby came the procedure was fairly similar. In my case we moved out to the country and certain elements changed. But basically, the dynamic was the same. Now the baby occupied most of my attention but the inward emphasis continued. Seldom did I have intelligent conversations as I had earlier. I occasionally listened to the radio. I felt isolated from life. Fears tumbled in and a loss of confidence followed. The previous inward brooding and isolation sow seeds of revolt in this 28-35 stage. What is experienced in this period is the dawning of discomfort, the sense of loss, the fear of change. There is no way to explain the shock of comparing oneself before and after the period of 'housewifing'. The fact that being a mother is very important and purposeful work only highlights the fact that great support is needed to go through this time creatively. The result of this feeling is often a strong sense of hostility because the husband is seen as the cause or at least the wife feels inadequate next to him at the very same time she is seeing all his faults and weaknesses. So the wife feels cheated and resentful.

In her book *The Brothers' System for Liberated Love and Marriage*, Dr. Joyce Brothers addresses herself to this problem. "Marriage can be liberated to meet the needs of women today, to preserve the love and cherishing and excitement while discarding the restrictive and damaging aspects of the relationship."[27] She points out that the power of love is so strong at the beginning of marriage that the woman accepts a one-sided view of herself even though it is hurting her. If a change toward equality can be effected both partners have so much more to gain from an equal partnership of marriage. "The answer is not to abolish marriage but to liberate it – a loving union in which each partner is as concerned about promoting the happiness and growth and fulfilment of the other as he or she is about promoting his or her own happiness, growth and fulfilment." In chapter 5, Brothers goes on to suggest ways in which a woman can change her view of herself, usually by cultivating a strong interest, doing part or full time work, regaining self-respect, and in most cases becoming much more interesting to herself and to her husband, opening herself up to a larger circle of people and the resulting stimulation. Can this be done while one is trying to be a conscientious full-time mother? If one is careful in planning it can be done. It is not easy, but it must happen if the woman feels the need for it. She cannot wait five years to become a person again. But she has to be realistic in the amount of time she can spend.

A woman has to be careful about fooling herself. I have known too many 'full-time' mothers who spend a great deal of their time leaving their children with babysitters while they pursue this or that, deluding themselves that they are really spending time with their children. It would be simpler to have a regularly scheduled time for babysitting so that she could take a class, pursue a specific training, or work for a particular length of time.

The question of full-time work is a very individual situation, and I am not suggesting this is the answer. It may be in certain circumstances due to finances, the particular person's needs, or the way the couple can work out parenting schedules. The value of mothering cannot be stressed enough, but the guilt that is felt if one is not parenting full time (regardless of the quality) needs to be considered. Another aspect to consider here is the relationhip with grandparents or older friends for whom babysitting might be meaningful both for child and adult. I had a wonderful situation one year when my children were 6 months - 1 year and 3-4 years old. The 60 year old mother of a friend of mine and I worked out a mutual arrangement. I left my children with her twice a week for 2 hours while I tutored. Not only did it work out nicely for them, but the older woman enjoyed serving me a cup of tea when I returned. It brought her companionship as well as knowing that she had helped me. I often think back to that time and the value we all received.

There are other ways of gaining strength during these periods. Making sure that one has private time of one's own sometime everyday is very helpful. Whether one uses it for reading, thinking, studying, meditating or artwork, it should be inwardly very active; a special moment in a busy day in which a woman learns to be alone with herself. The beauty of solitude is healing and helps her to develop sensitive qualities.

Choosing one area of interest and pursuing it over a period of time can also be very helpful and it serves to focus the woman's thoughts from the general distractions of her day. Everything in the woman's life fights concentration. Her energies are continually dissipated on the periphery which does not help her own sense of inferiority and inability to concentrate (a point often made when wives return to college, is that they are afraid of not being able to concentrate). She will often surprise herself and find that she has become knowledgeable in an area, and has developed professional expertise.

The desert land which is often felt during this period is fertile ground for problems. A third person may enter the relationship. The 'other woman' fortifies the husband's masculinity. She offers him adoration and builds up his ego. The man who has not resolved the earlier feeling period with mature judgment seeks approval from others. He cannot make sound judgment of himself and wants to escape from the self examination which is needed if he is to use the rational soul capacities to their utmost. Whereas the woman in this predicament will look for 'romance' the man is looking for a woman who will make him feel 'more of a man' rather than less of a man as he really feels himself to be. Gone is the strong love of passionate youth but now such a man will use the woman in a parasitic way for his own egoistic satisfaction.

He doesn't set out to do this consciously. He is as confused about himself as the woman who becomes frantic in her need to justify her existence by trying each new thing. He lacks the passion and tenderness of youth and has not yet gained the real feeling of the other person that should be growing during this time. He is aware of his own needs and sees the other person as an object to supply his need. The woman in this case is often feeling desperate to be wanted and takes part in the triangle. Unknowingly they use each other in a destructive way.

I remember some powerful dreams during these years of life. In the midst of crisis I dreamt that up until this time we had been puppets on strings. But then the puppeteers let go and we collapsed. We were now free to move by ourselves. In the dream the puppeteers looked at us and said, "It's your turn now and you're not doing too well". In the same night I dreamed there was a great green valley, then dry brown parched plains, and in the distance rich green foothills. As I look back I see the validity of that picture. At that period it was one of the few aspects of hope I experienced.

The crisis period during this desert time can take on another form. The man can show excessive interest and desire to help another person, particularly a woman. He puts out enormous efforts on her behalf and dwells in self-sacrifice. He sees himself as a knight, gives time, attention and consideration in a way he has not given his wife since he courted her. What he is really doing is stirring up self-pity, feeling self-satisfaction for his noble deeds. He convinces himself that he is irreplaceable. Many women long for this attention from other men since their husbands are not providing it. Both wallow in self-pity.

Whereas the man concentrates on outer physical deeds, the woman often makes the attempt to look inside herself and find out what is going on. She senses something independent of her surroundings, something changing within herself which has made her feel ill at ease, dissatisfied, cynical and terribly lonely. The task of this period is to develop independent judgment and understanding of another human being. This capacity needs solitude. Rudolf Steiner characterises the period from 30-33 as analogous to the last three years of Christ's life. It is in effect a death experience in which one goes through the valley of the shadow of death. During this period one learns what it is like to be without friends, that whatever friendships one has should be between equals, rather than one person being powerful. It is very important to have friends during this time, but to learn not to depend on them is also important. It becomes more and more evident that one cannot help another person until one really knows oneself as a person and respects oneself. The pathway to growth is to recognise the other person as one who is on the same path as oneself, equally capable of freedom, not by making other people dependent.

During this period a business-like approach begins to operate in marriage. Strong diversities in temperament show up. Views and lifestyles weigh heavier.

If the earlier differences are not lovingly reconciled, estrangement and withdrawal become more pronounced. ("I'll have to adjust to the relationship by doing my own work.") The shimmer of romantic love begins to vanish. Sex has become routine, something deeper has to arise to prevent the relationship from becoming commonplace. When the couple is able to separate the essential from the unessential, to open up the eye for the individuality of the other, new faculties emerge which result in warm companionship and trust. This can develop into a deeper meeting with the other, leading to a true love based on spiritual encounter.

During this period there are many opportunities for cooperation, particularly as the family is growing. Planning for a holiday, or remodeling a house together while the marriage itself is falling apart is not unusual.

The critical challenge is set during the thirties. Either the couple can make this step in growth or there will be a major marriage crisis in the forties. So many positive aspects come out of this intellectual period, which if worked through can stimulate growth. Both the ability to see the pros and cons and matter-of-factness can provide the basis for an acceptance of one's fellow being as he is. The ability to understand begins to grow, to strive towards truth, to learn to face oneself in aloneness. The seeds of selfless love develop. But each person has his own time frame. Some refuse to take the necessary steps to develop these new capacities. Instead one may want to live in the past. When we see people in their late thirties living like twenty year olds they seem sentimental and foolish. They hold onto romantic love and keep searching for deep and passionate love. The person mourns the loss of the old feeling of being beloved, of experiencing the hot blush of newness, the thrill. This loss is experienced as death.

If two people have shared years of marriage but have failed to communicate both the joys and sorrows, an atmosphere of reproach can occur. Trust built over years of working together can bring deep joy. But if trust is not there, it is seldom possible to open someone's eyes to the being of another. Marriage reflects inner development of the partners and can only mature if they can develop towards a full humanness. The first step in this development is accepting oneself, is self-knowledge. Otherwise one is deadlocked. Part of growing is developing one's personality more strongly, and differentiation intensifies. But in marriage the one can strengthen the other. "A complete sharing between two people is an impossibility and whenever it seems, nevertheless, to exist, it is a narrowing, a mutual agreement which robs both members of full freedom and development. But, once the realization is accepted that even between the closest human beings, infinite distances continue to exist, a wonderful living side by side can grow up, if they succeed in loving the distance between them which makes it possible for each to see the other whole and against a wide sky."[28]

I remember a conversation with a friend I hadn't seen in a while. We were catching up on where we were in our marriages. She was telling me how often she found herself apologising or explaining for her husband. She didn't know why, she could just see the little places where he irritated someone or caused annoyance. Finally one evening a friend told her, "Lay off Lyn, you're his wife, not his analyst." She said that rather than being annoyed, she was relieved. Then she was shocked at her own arrogance. What had given her the right to judge him? I don't think she is alone. One of the problems that does occur in marriages, particularly ones that have been going for quite a while, is the feeling that you know the other person very well and you need to protect people from his faults.

There comes a point in a relationship, and in this case it can be a close friendship as well as a marriage, when one lets go. One no longer asks why am I with this person, or sees their faults, or adds up the irritations, marking them in some invisible account book. There comes the point where all that disappears and one acknowledges: this person is my husband, this person is my friend, and I accept him or her totally. At that point one can begin to work on the relationship in a different way. Now one can understand, give, commit, allowing new forces of warmth and support to develop.

Another intrusion into this difficult time can be the mingling of spiritual and physical realities in egoistic love for its own sake. Here love does not exist for the sake of the beloved but for the lover. This feeling can be uplifting and beautiful but it has a shallow side too. Self-will enters. For the spiritual world love must evolve through the person's development, permeated with inner strength and self-improvement. This progression then spreads in rippling circles. We cannot really love rightly if we have not developed a love for all mankind, for nature, for the self. In summing up this period, the thrust is for balance. If the woman has been in the working world she often yearns to settle down and have children, to be at home. If she has been home she wants to move outward. Both have transitional problems, both call for a new relationship with one's partner. Although the character of the problems will differ depending on which side of the scales the woman finds herself, the inner nature is the same. The way we seek balance may be clumsy, awkward, strange. It is almost always painful, but as Andre Lourde states so graphically, "Pain will always either change or stop".[29]

Gail Sheehy describes this as a period of reappraisal. If the person is married she will question the commitment. If the person is single, she begins to look for marriage. The inner life takes on as much strength as the outer demands. An unseen unknowing force is rising from within like a silent volcano which will erupt in some cases, spill out in weak spots in others. A despairing recognition that comes during this time is that our intellect cannot answer all the questions of life.

In a couple who marry over 30 there is a somewhat different experience. Their ideas are more formed, their habits more set, each has his own circle of friends, career interest. These people tend to respect each other in the idea realm more easily. Neither has formed the other. They come as two entities. There is more need and more possibility for respect and freedom. Issues are talked out. Second marriages tend to follow this pattern as well.

The Valley of the Shadow - 35-42

Before considering this period and its relation to marriage as a totality I would like to pause and look at the 35th year itself. We must consider what each partner is experiencing. The 35th year is described as the cosmic midnight of the soul, the great crisis in life. Gail Sheehy characterises it in this way, "I have reached some sort of meridian in my life. I had better take a survey, re-examine where I have been, and re-evaluate how I am going to spend my resources from now on. Why am I doing all this? What do I really believe in? Underneath this vague feeling is the fact, as yet unacknowledged, that there is a down side to life, a back of the mountain, and that I have only so much time before the dark to find my own truth . . . (these thoughts) usher in a decade that can be called, in the deepest sense, the Deadline Decade. Somewhere between 35 and 45 if we let ourselves, most of us will have a full-out authenticity crisis."[30]

This also could be described as a time of doubt. One must go through this period, there is no turning back. Doubt of everything settles in. The will is paralyzed, one feels rudderless, there is a lack of ease, loss of faculty of memory, a real absence of inner light. This is beautifully shown in Thomas Cole's painting *Middle Age*. If this period is transcended the person continues and experiences the helplessness of the soul. This experience needs to be deeply lived through or it recurs until it is met and resolved. If one gets through it well, a new lease on life is felt. A new sense of power is realized, the lost faculties return with a new quality. Memory feels strengthened and the personality is under much greater control of the ego.

This is described in Steiner's terms as the birth of the consciousness soul. It is a time when we begin to look at life more passively, to allow knowledge to be revealed to us rather than pushing aggressively to acquire knowledge. Persons and things can now speak to us and be perceived in their true nature in the absence of egoism. This has a strong effect on relationships. It allows the person to withdraw the self before the presence of the other so that the inner nature of that person can speak. This person begins to develop a sense of who she is, the worth of her own being, and potential. This security brings with it the supreme gift of selfless love. She has everything she needs and does not need to get it from another person. What she gets from others in a relationship will be a gift from them which she can gladly accept. I emphasise these words because they are a signpost on the path of life.

We constantly have to come back to it but at least we know that back on the twisting path there was a sign. We only have to find our way to it again and pick up from there.

So this birth of the ego has to do with freedom, and it is the ego that determines development in life. "Freedom means choosing your burden. You can exchange one burden for another, but you must carry one. If you don't carry a burden, you don't know who you are."[31]

What is the 35 year old like? Here we see the great dichotomy. Often the 35 year old woman is still asking for an allowance. She spends dull days killing time. She doesn't know what she wants to believe in anymore. She isn't sure she likes her children, usually because she isn't sure she likes herself. At the same time she wants to push herself into the world. "Let me in. I want to be smart and important and have value placed on my time and talents too. Is it possible to pick up where I stopped learning? Do men still find me appealing? I wish someone would take me seriously. I wish someone would help me stop being afraid."

What about the 35 year old man? Time is running out. He feels that if he doesn't hurry and become successful he'll be a failure. He loses faith in his ideas as he has to compromise himself to advance. He can't even count on himself sexually anymore. Inwardly he feels tender, isolated, dependent, outwardly he feels vain and greedy, jealous and competitive. He doesn't always want to be expected to be the strong one. He feels panic as strongly as she feels fear. Is it any wonder that marriages at this time go through chaos?

The only answer in both the case of the man and the woman is self examination. One has to let go of fantasy projection on the other. If one held on to the projection through the early thirties, one must finally let go and separate oneself. A sense of survival often pushes us ahead into the dark world we fear. We have to find an honest unity in ourselves.

During the second half of life we possess only what we have developed in the first half. But now we can use this in a conscious way whereas before we were too often oppressed by our emotions to allow the ego individuality to work through them. All through life we get glimpses of our own destiny. Sometimes we try to fight this glimpse, at other times we welcome it because it affirms our own intuitions. When we grasp these occasional glimpses we are able to see a broader picture of our life. Then it is often possible for us to accept a relationship to friends and/or a marriage partner even when it is uncomfortable. We become more understanding of family members, more loyal to our friends, and more loving to our mate. Once one becomes sure of this the whole perspective on the relationship changes. One knows one is there to stay, come heaven or hell. One has to work certain things out, but there is a karmic tie and certain traits to be worked with. Often a new patience develops; the little details become important, the thoughtful little moments that do not come out of duty but out of free will. Hephzibah Menuhin Hauser describes "the tremendous and unequal division between the discipline imposed from the outside and the purely intuitive self-willing that came from choice. I learned that real responsibility has to do with what you choose to do. You can do the most difficult things all your life and they are worthwhile, if for no other reason than that you have chosen them freely. We have come to the wrong conclusion if you think that if you get rid of what is bad for you and what you hate, then you will be okay. Yes, we have got to get rid of what is bad, but at the same time we have to know what we are going to use our freedom for."[32]

As individuals begin to work this through, they cultivate the ability to recognise opportunities for helping, the right moment for action. Perception is heightened as is sense of timing. Life becomes a great adventure in living because it is not centred on needs and demands of the self. The question now becomes whether to use this new released power for the self or for the world.

At the crossroads we experience loss of youth. We look in the mirror and the changes astound us. As we notice hair appearing on the chin, or looseness of skin around the neck, we are surprised because we thought it couldn't happen to us. When our parents were 40 they looked so old. But here we are ourselves. Remember when we thought everyone over 30 was over the hill. This is a time of the double edged sword – danger and opportunity. All of us have the chance to rework the narrow identity by which we defined ourselves in the first half of life and this can lead to a full catharsis. To come through this we must re-examine our purpose and re-evaluate how to spend our strength and talents. No matter what we have been doing, there will be parts of ourselves that have been suppressed and now need to find expression. Bad feelings will demand acknowledgment along with the good. Along the way we will find that we are alone. We no longer have to ask permission because we are now the providers of our own safety. We now must learn to give ourselves permission. This is difficult, particularly for women. We stumble upon the feminine or masculine aspects of our natures that up to now have been masked. We become afraid of their being exposed to our partners.

Another characteristic of this period is the feeling of grief in the dreams of dying, the sense of the old self passing away. One may dream of one's partner dying and feel guilt at the thought. But what is really happening is that part of oneself is dying. By taking in our suppressed and even our unwanted parts we prepare at the gut level for the reintegration of an identity that is ours and ours alone. Our personality really becomes our own. We are not a patchwork quilt of our culture, there to please those around us. We can truly become interesting people. But this is a process that needs time.

A couple is in for serious trouble when either separately or together they cannot find new spiritual content in their lives. If they can experience new purpose in their relationship and become conscious of their struggle they may experience new aims in their lives. There is no escape from the reality of the middle aged years even though alcohol, drugs and sexual encounters may be used to dull the pain. No one can regain his youth, but a new attitude can help. If this new attitude has to do with human relationships in the context of spiritual understanding, there is much significant work ahead. Once one glimpses one's mate as a spiritual entity a remarkable experience occurs. This grows out of a religious vision or an ideological conviction of a deep rooted trust in the ego of that person.

One of the characteristics of this period is dealing with negative experiences. Whereas in the previous soul period one could see the faults of the mate, the experience now intensifies. It is almost as if a caricature emerges so that the positive qualities are distorted and the negative qualities loom into the foreground. We get to know what is called the 'double' of our mate and it tricks us and we find ourselves unknowingly doing or saying things we will regret or things that we hardly believe we are doing. Our own double leads us into the vicious and self destructive act over and over again even though we know the outcome of this confrontation. In fact, we get to know the other person's 'double' far better than our own. The significant change comes when we learn to observe how we act on others and how our own good intentions are repeatedly misunderstood. We keep 'coming across' to others incorrectly. Then we feel rejected. "Why don't others see us as we really are?" "Why can't they see what we mean?" When we begin to look at this we will see our own doubles and stop concentrating on our partner's which is so obvious to us. The moment we consciously face this is the turning point in our development individually and as a couple. If we work through this, trust and caring as great healing powers will be released. One then can become attentive to the personality of the other, to be able to know and love it.

This inner crossroad is often sensed by women before men experience it. But both partners want to avoid facing it whenever it does come. There is an unconscious sense that facing it will require inner change. Some men respond to these inner changes by throwing themselves fully into work or constant activity. He discovers he has been too anxious to please and too vulnerable to criticism. Now he wants to put everything together on his own ship. He feels restless, stale, burdened and unappreciated. He may depart from long time commitments, including marriage. He may choose a second career. He may be self-destructive. At the same time strong feelings of tenderness are aroused and he may be more interested in the ethical aspect of life.

For a woman who stands at this point she often feels "I loved being a mother, a housewife. But I never really felt cherished. Why doesn't someone appreciate me?" That's where she sees the problem. The assertive woman who has found herself will say "It took me too long, too much psychic sweat to get where I am emotionally and professionally. I'm not about to let someone erode that. Life is too short so I'll stay alone for a while. There are worse things than being alone." Out of this a new perspective on life and a new self-awareness is felt. This is quite different from the earlier attitude of dependence.

Taking Hold - emergence from the abyss - 40-50

The consciousness soul period extends from 35 to somewhere in the mid-forties at which time a new equilibrium is regained. If this has not happened the couple can look forward to having an even bigger crisis aound 50, but this time it will be a greater shock. However, if it is confronted whenever it comes, there can be a new attitude towards life. A new purpose for living is experienced: "I cannot expect anyone to understand me. I am just learning to understand myself." Once one has this attitude, one is more forgiving of the partner, there is a new warmth, a relaxation. The man begins to experience more of the feminine in himself which allows him to appreciate his wife. The woman has to grasp this new quality in her husband and support it. Although there is a wisdom in this tenderness it can sometimes disarm, especially in a man who had previously been tough and aggressive. A loyalty may be born during this period which deepens the love relationship, reaching beyond death and remaining positive no matter what happens. Often such a relationship born in the thirties will with long and careful tending become adult in the fifties. This is a giving form of love.

Friends become very important in relationships. So does privacy. The couple feels the time for impressing each other is over and they want to be straight and direct.

This is a time for discovering the emotional parts of oneself that did not fit in with the previous picture that each was trying to protect. The awakening of the man to the gentleness he had previously only allowed himself to love in the woman is a powerful experience. He is often fascinated by this and begins to explore it the way a young woman does in her twenties. He becomes more interested in his home, in gardening, in cooking, art, music. Now he wants to live by his feelings. This opens up the wonderful potential of dialogue with his wife, especially if he becomes conscious of what is happening. Because for the first time they have a truly shared emotional experience, the relationship deepens further. The danger in this period is that the woman who becomes too involved with her own masculine side will push away the feminine in him as soft. He is like a tender flower just opening and he may have some questions about it. She must leave room for this and not intimidate him. A man who has cultivated artistic activities throughout his thirties will not have as strong a contrast in this new experience. There is a loving vulnerability in men of this age who are struggling to express tenderness and caring. This vulnerability makes some men very appealing. For a young woman who begins a relationship with a man this age there is the potential for a deep bond which will flower for a number of years until she comes into her own thirties and starts being assertive. He will dote on her and she will love the love that is surrounding her. It comes from the inner core of his own being; it is not selfish. For her in her twenties it is selfish and she will use it to her own advantage, sometimes making a fool of the older man. In Ingmar Bergman's *Scenes from a Marriage* we have this quality in Johan.

In the case of a wife who has been victimized by her husband's previous strength, this change will be difficult. The man had not appreciated her qualities, was caught up in aggressiveness, didn't share his experiences with her. She has become removed and resentful of his lack of attention. Now he awakens to his new self and wants to express it. When he yearns for companionship and gentleness he no longer finds it in his mate and becomes demanding and hurt. She has deep hostility built up. It is easy for her to say "When I valued those qualities you cut me apart, you weren't there. Now you want this experience and I am embittered and hard. It is your fault. If you had only known then what you know now, we would have been so happy. Now it is too late." This is not an uncommon situation. For the woman the temptation to lose herself in 'I told you so' is great. But it is just now that she has to look deeply into herself and face her own attitudes. She is usually feeling a new sense of security and her man's need for her strengthens that. If she is not careful she can become callous and thoughtless and so miss a wonderful time of companionship.

It is during this period that the couple can see marriage as an art form, as the most challenging and complex of all works a human being can be inspired to create. They experience that this marriage form is never complete. The couple now have the perspective to see that marriage is of their own making. They must take responsibility for it as a labour of love. This is the most critical turning point in marriage and cannot be emphasised strongly enough. If this is not consciously grasped, the marriage may have been good but may also reach a natural end. They do not see that whatever happens from here on depends on their own energy and resolve. Some couples try to make a change through prayer. Others resort to attempts to awaken the other which only become nagging. If we concentrate on waiting for the

other to change, nothing occurs but bitterness. We have to take the
first step and change in ourselves not for an end goal, but because we
have faced ourselves and see the need for the change. We cannot start
the change and expect recognition. As long as we see ourselves as
victims of a marriage, change will not occur. When we learn that what
we receive in time, service or material things from our partners are
unselfish gifts, we can begin a living marriage. We begin to value pain
as the teacher of new capacities. This is a time when marriages bear
obvious differences. The maturity of a marriage is like the face of an
old person. Everything is 'out front'. The scars, the joys, the fears, the
tenderness on the soul level. For those who have met the challenge in a
loving way there results a higher level of understanding, a greater
satisfaction. For others there are many compromises and adjustments
which are less satisfactory but in spite of the disillusionment the
marriage goes on. Perhaps this is most common. For others the earlier
stress period marked the beginning of a series of crises, resulting in
progressive deterioration until divorce is the final outcome.

Most couples survive a series of crises before divorcing. Rigidity
and flexibility play in to the situation. If the couple lacks flexibility
divorce is seen as a quick answer, whereas if a couple values
adjustment and is more flexible, there is a chance of resolution of the
conflict.

The Deepening Experience - 49-56

By the time the couple enters this phase, middle age is a fact of life. The persons have re-established and relaxed. Values are seen from a different perspective. The strong urge to compete has been severely lessened. In this period there emerges a great freedom – the freedom to reform oneself, to be independent in a relationship, to live out of one's own values rather than society's expectations. What has one come through to reach this period?

There has been a critical reassessment of goals and outer success in relation to one's own well being. This reassessment is characterised, particularly with men, as middlescence. One of the most common symptoms which follows is the career change as part of a total life style change. In the case of a successful person, he or she has discovered that success has not brought happiness, so what is really worthwhile in life? This is a crisis in itself. If the person has not achieved the dreams of his youth he has to face this and this too brings on a crisis. He has to deal with the question of whether or not life is worth living at all. For some this is the time when commitments are broken because they decide to live life to its fullest and at least get some enjoyment out of it.

The world becomes very grey. He sees that if he has been successful it has been bought at a price. His colleagues, his family may not really appreciate him. He begins to face his behaviour of the past where he justified everything in the name of success. He may wish to re-establish connections with his children, to make up for the lack of relationship earlier, and that does not always meet with instant support. Once the success goal is released there is a great empty space. As the person develops he finds new capacities of feeling filling this space. At first this is unknown and strange but then he feels its fullness and experiences the joys of caring for other people.

The role change cannot be over-emphasised. For women, it often comes more naturally, especially if her first career of housewife has been ended by the children leaving home. After she survives that crisis and starts doing something about her life, she may begin to establish her second phase, by returning to school, finding a job, starting a business or volunteering for community work. In most cases, once she has overcome the fears she will be accepted by society in principle. However, many women go through great stress because they have nothing of value to show after 20 years at home. Their skills are outdated, often companies are not interested in women in their fifties, particularly since they are fighting weight problems, wrinkles, health problems, or heavy responsibilities at home. We have to re-evaluate this aspect in society at large. These women cannot compete with 'go-getters' in their twenties, but they bring a sense of stability into the business world that is healing.

For the man or woman who has pursued a career for twenty years or so, it may now seem stale. New ideas abound, usually the change is toward a role more oriented to deeper interests than money and success; a secret hobby, an artistic or outdoor interest, or a caring profession. Occasionally, this necessitates more schooling or retraining at a time when the man feels his intellectual faculties waning. He has proved himself in the world and now has to do it again where he is insecure. He needs a great deal of support, particularly if the risk involves considerable financial loss. This is a difficult situation for many families today. The man who has been providing a particular life style now decides to change careers. The family follows the change and may undergo a radical adjustment. The house may be sold, holidays disappear, family savings are used for living so that other choices become limited. The children usually are most affected by this if they are still living at home. They are often confused by the changes in their father and are called on to be supportive and sympathetic at a time when they are (understandably) selfishly thinking of their own lives. It is a strong wife who can keep her family together at this time, nurturing her husband's change and introducing new values to the children which may affect their own lives.

Today we have also the reverse phenomena happening. The woman decides she must pursue a new direction. The family, particularly the husband, has to go through the necessary life changes. Some husbands are now faced with changing their career or place of work in order to keep their marriage. The home situation changes. Everyone has to do more chores, since the wife and mother has changed her life. A woman or man who has gone through a family breakup has been shocked out of the day-in-day-out assumptions of life and now begins to look at new possibilities.

It is also very possible that just as the husband is going through his career change, the wife is also preparing for a new life. The dynamics of this will also have a strong effect on the marriage. It can be a very supportive team as each is going into new territory, they can share their fears and comfort each other. He can be proud of her excitement at a time when he can experience his own uncertainties.

"Both partners are lost in a common sea of the universal which absorbs and yet frees, which separates and yet unites. Is this now what the mature relationship, the meeting of two solitudes is meant to be?"[33]

The Free Gift - coming of age - 56-63 and beyond

When one looks at marriage in the later years, in the late 50s and 60s and beyond, one finds another quality emerging as prevalent – that of devotion. The depth and richness of devotion is a metamorphosis of early love which sheds a radiance in later life. There is a depth to the love of partners at this period that can barely be experienced in the earlier years when we are so much more outwardly-oriented. Appreciation and tolerance are also qualities that characterise our later years.

Older people are looking back and yet looking forward. The pace seems slower, and there is more time for reflection. If they are vital and alive, interested in life, they continue to grow and stimulate those around them. If, however, they have not faced earlier crises they get locked in and repeat certain behaviour patterns over and over again. There is cynicism and bitterness about unresolved hopes and dreams. In retirement couples are faced with the reality of endless time together. Are they really prepared for it?

I have seen elderly people who are some of the most exciting human beings I know. They continue to live life with interest and wonder. A number are doing very creative work in their 70s, writing, speaking, teaching. They have a lifetime of experience to share through insights and intuitions, and they have little to gain in terms of ambition by the work they now do. But they continue to give.

Companionship is probably the most powerful element of the marital relationship during this time. Friendship with those old friends with whom one has built a reservoir of communication and experience is another strength of older years. Friendship is the key to the age of life regardless of sex or marital situation. One evening we had dinner in a café in San Francisco. Behind, in the next booth were three men in their late 60s. Their conversation was fascinating. I could hear certain patterns that seemed well formed, phrases that repeated themselves. But they understood each other so well and they were such a strong support to each other, that I was deeply moved. Their lively conversation was a marked contrast to the effort it took them to put on their jackets and coats, scarves and hats. The minds were vital and young, the bodies were rigid and worn. The strength of their friendship was a solid bond.

I recently read the dual autobiography of Will and Ariel Durant and was impressed with their reflection on their long marriage and working relationship. Following are a few quotes:

After 40 years of marriage Will wrote, "Everything here is conducive to quiet composition, but I find that your absence leads me to sit and mope for minutes at a time; I would be less distracted by your gossipy talks over the phone . . . Come home as soon as you can."[34]

After 52 years of marriage, "I note from Will's diary that at Chicago he took for his subject the 'Evolution of Love'. I know the lecture; it was a frank tracing of the development of sex in the plant and animal world; the historical embellishment of physical relations with the psychological results of female retreat and feminine modesty; male idealization of the desired and refused object; aesthetic feelings and romantic sentiment; and finally, the mutual solicitude and devotion that come not from the erotic desire but from long and faithful comradeship."[35]

On their 57th anniversary, Will wrote, "Today, October 31, 1970, is the fifth-seventh anniversary of our marriage. On November 5 I shall be eighty-five, not old enough to be a sage, but ready to finish this book and my life. I speak only for myself. Ariel is still in full vigor and spirit. . . My greatest blessing now is her continued presence. The sound of her slippered feet moving swiftly about the house is a comforting obligate assuring constancy. When she sits down to work or talk with me she is a bubbling fount of inspiration and insight . . . All in all I have had a happy life; I am grateful for it, and would be glad to live it again."[36]

Nena O'Neil was comparing marriages today with young and middle-aged people, then looking at her own parents. She was amazed and touched at the difference in old-fashioned marriage values from what so many of us experience today. She was reflecting on a situation where her mother's health was holding her father back from a trip he had anticipated for a long time. "But she says it without conviction. She doesn't have to say that she is sorry for holding him back. She expects his devotion and he gives it, not out of guilt, not out of duty, but out of love. She cared for him and devoted her life to the family through all their lean years, scrubbing and cooking and ironing in the normal way, now it is his turn to care for her. They have cared for and taken care of each other throughout their married lives, and now it is no different. This is simply what marriage is for them. The things done for one another, the love, are not accounts to be balanced daily;

caring and love and obligations are evened out over the long years of a lifetime."[37]

Is our problem today that we cannot see as long as a lifetime? We want the return now!

This touches on the question of permanence which forms such a block in our relationships. We tend to physicalize time, we want everything to last forever, to imprison the moments and possess them. It bothers us that romantic love does not persist in the same form in later years. It is with pain we realise that you cannot love someone every moment in the same way, that relationships go through birth, death and rebirth. We resist this transformation. We want it to be the same predictable way. We fight freedom in its truest sense, growth. We try to possess and hold the golden moment but it slips out of our fingers and transforms itself like a will o' the wisp. We long for security, but find there is none. We have to value the moment, appreciate it when it comes, and prepare for the future. But we cannot fix the future. Life is far too fluid and interesting to fit the mould, any mould.

We have passed through the periods of individual life and relationship. From the dreamer we have spun our dreams, coated with sentimentality and optimism. The shock of waking up shook the dream dust from our eyes and prodded us with doubt and judgment. With some warning the path descended downward into the valley of the shadow of death, we have tumbled into the abyss, some of us head first, others sliding down along the edge fighting all the way. Once one has hit bottom, the spark of light shines from the distance. Some of us see the spark and take hold working our way out. Others stay in the abyss for a long time. Once having emerged from the abyss life has a different character, it has become deeper, richer, more precious. We look to ourselves for the cause of unhappiness, and what is more important we begin to take the first steps. We begin a pilgrimage to the essence of life, to the other, to the self. We learn to offer ourselves as a gift and to receive the other as a gift. We learn to say, How can I be of help to you? How can I serve? In other words we offer ourselves in communion with life, is this not the true marriage of spirit? As we renew our vow of marriage and fidelity to the being of the other we make it real and joyous, we accept the scars and the laugh lines, for we have helped to create them. Our relationship becomes a free gift and the ripening fruit the harvest of our lives.

The faith in the other is the faith in ourselves, to acknowledge metamorphosis in human life, in nature, in all the universe, to grasp the key. Each step in metamorphosis is the bud of a new beginning, the step towards transcendence. The being emerges on a new level; love and growth become one, the one is the two, is the many. To know each other in love of friendship, in love of relationship is one of the reasons we were born.

Footnotes

1. Franklin L. Baumer, *Modern European Thought, Continuity and Change in Ideas 1600 - 1950*, Macmillan Publishing, New York 1977, p.20.

2. André Lourde, *Interview with the Muse*, Broadside Press, Detroit 1977, p.79.

3. Rollo May, *Man's Search for Himself*, The New American Library Inc., New York 1967, p.206.

4. Rudolf Steiner, *The Spiritual Beings in the Heavenly Bodies and in the Kingdom of Nature*, R. Steiner Publishing, London 1951, pp.51-52.

5. Bernard Lievegoed, *Towards the 21st Century, Doing the Good*, Rudolf Steiner Publications, Toronto 1983.

6. Note on Archangels – Nine heavenly hierarchies have special tasks in bringing about the evolution of the cosmos, earth and humanity. The Angels are nearest to the souls of men, the guardians of individual human beings. The next closest hierarchy is that of the Archangels who are deeply connected with the leadership of a people, language, the nation. Rudolf Steiner mentioned seven Archangels who guide broad movements in civilization in successive periods of about 320 years each. Each Archangel has a different influence. Since 1879 Michael has been the ruling Archangel, influencing people through their thinking to feel a common humanity that goes beyond race, nation or class. Before the time of Michael, Gabriel ruled from the 16th to the 19th centuries working through people's feelings to influence their connection with the family or national group.

7. James Stephens, *Crock of Gold*, Collier Books, New York 1972, pp.111-112.

8. Ibid.

9. Ibid.

10. Lesley Hazelton, *Israeli Women, The Reality Behind the Myths*, Simon and Schuster, New York 1977.

11. Padraic Colum includes this myth in his book, *Myths of the World,* and refers to it as a Jewish-Post Christian myth. Hazelton footnotes it as coming from the Alpha Beta di Ben Sira, an alphabetically arranged Mishnaic commentary written sometime before the eleventh century. She says, "The author of the Alpha Beta drew on early Hebrew legends arising from the discrepancy between the accounts of creation in the first two chapters of Genesis. In the first, man and woman are created

simultaneously, on the sixth day of creation. In the second, woman is created as an afterthought, so that man shall not be lonely. The discrepancy is attributed to a careless weaving together of early Judaean and later rabbinical tradition."

12. Hazelton, p.112.

13. Ibid, pp.113-114.

14. Hazelton p.115, citing from Robert Graves and Raphael Patai, *Hebrew Myths, the Book of Genesis*, McGraw-Hill 1966.

15. Herb Goldberg, *The Hazards of being Male, Surviving the Myth of Masculine Privilege*, A Signet Book, New American Library, New York 1977.

16. Steiner, *Philosophy of Freedom*, Rudolf Steiner Press, London 1970, p.205.

17. Jessie Bernard, *The Future of Marriage*, World Publishing Co., New York 1972, pp.38-39, citing William Congreve, *The Way of the World*.

18. Ibid, p.42, citing Philip Slater, *What hath Spock Wrought?* Washington Post, 1 March 1970.

19. Wendell Berry, *The Unsettling of America; Culture and Agriculture*, Sierra Club Books, San Francisco 1977, p.113.

20. Ibid, p.117.

21. Jessie Bernard, p.48.

22. Anne Morrow Lindbergh, *Gift from the Sea*, Pantheon Books Inc., 1955, p.46-47.

23. Ibid, p.47.

24. Bernard, p.22.

25. This realm of emotion, instinct and feeling may be known as the 'sentient soul' period. Later development of more rational, thinking qualities may be called a time of 'intellectual soul'. Finally, the 'consciousness soul' period is a time of meeting ego-to-ego in the highest sense of work-to-be-done for contribution to the world itself.

26. Gail Sheehy, *Passages, Predictable Crises of Adult Life*, Bantam Edition, published by arrangement with E. P. Dutton & Co. 1977.

27. Dr. Joyce Brothers, *The Brothers System for Liberated Love and Marriage*, P. H. Weyden 1972.

28. Lindbergh, quoting Rilke, pp.97-98.

29. André Lourde, *From the Muse*, Broadside Press, Detroit 1973.

30. Sheehy, p.350.

31. Hephzibah Menuhin Hauser, *Interview with the Muse: Remarkable Women Speak on Creativity and Power*, Moon Books, Ca., distributed by Random House.

32. Hauser, p.40.

33. Lindbergh, p.107.

34. Durant, Will and Ariel, *A Dual Autobiography*, Simon and Schuster, New York 1977, p.305.

35. Ibid, p.318.

36. Ibid, pp.401-402

37. Nena O'Neil, *The Marriage Premise*, personal recollections.

Woman and Man
polarity and balance

Margli Matthews

To The Lady

Here I am. There
is the grass outside
and the wide sky;

and you are involved somehow.

It's not a vision I ask for.
Something simpler. Some apprehension
of your glance within this green.

You are a woman certainly. I've seen
where you would have been
if I'd looked a moment sooner.

Lady without footprint.

The slight lean of your head
co-incides
with how a bough bends
and makes it girlish.

How you laugh the light.

But sometimes I have found you
in the night side of a leaf –
a grief without eyelids.

Lady I would name you in grass and flower
and speak no word about the Spirit.

Paul Matthews

The Search for the New Feminine

Coming to the question of our search for balance now, in the mid 1980s, I would say that more men and women are involved in this than even seven years ago and that there is a greater urgency to the quest now. There is also a growing understanding that the outer manifestations of imbalance around us (in this case looked at in terms of the feminine and masculine polarity) are a reflection of our own inner imbalances, the disharmony in our relationships and the smaller circles of our lives. We begin to realize that in order to change the world we need to change ourselves, that the personal and the small determine the political and the universal. The growing Green Movement in England and Europe has been in part responsible for fostering this awareness. Within the Green Movement women particularly have brought this point home.

In recent years, more women have begun to link their struggle for liberation with other fundamental issues and questions of our time – questions of peace, ecology, unemployment, of health, medicine, the breakdown of family life, of the suffering and exploitation of the Third World, and the growing threat to humanity and the earth from nuclear power and nuclear weapons. As women have won a surer place and voice in the world, we have begun to wake up to the responsibilities that come with the freedom we have gained. We have looked towards our own inner balance and development, while at the same time concerning ourselves with the well-being of others and the need for social renewal; we have remembered our age-long connection to the being of the earth and our responsibility for her care and protection.

Behind this shift in awareness in women and the Women's Movement, has been the growing realisation that not only have women been excluded from life in the last centuries, but the feminine quality in all human beings has been undervalued and pushed out; that along with women this feminine principle needs to find new recognition and dignity, new value and expression. The need and quest for an awakened and transformed feminine to be brought into the life of our times has been one of the underlying aims of the Feminist Movement since the beginning of this century. However, this deeper purpose has not always been visible. In the last years this has begun to change and as women and men together strive to meet and find the feminine in the world and to unlock her in their souls, a new warmth and light, a new hope for balance begins to meet the forces of dark and cold, disharmony and imbalance that seem to grow stronger and more entrenched daily.

Increasingly, a sense for the wholeness and purpose, the meaning and mystery of life, is submerged by an abstract, mechanical view of the world and human beings. Through the development of science and technology, we have gained control over our lives and have acquired a vast knowledge about the universe, the earth and human beings as physical realities. But other realities have been excluded. Science and technology have been our highest goals, while conscience and individual moral imagination appear impossibly frail in the face of them. With our detached, intellectual consciousness, we have stripped the world and human beings of their inwardness – we have denied the inner being, the soul, of men and women, nature and the universe.

There is an ever widening gap between knowledge and understanding, between what we do and what we feel, what we think and who we are. Knowledge is no longer insight and understanding, but the accumulation of information and facts which we can possess, which gives us power and control but is not connected to morality and meaning and the imagination. We do not have to look far to see the consequences of this. Separated from a sense of oneness with Nature, we have long regarded her as something to be conquered and tamed, a resource to be used, consumed and exploited. Through our materialistic, scientific consciousness, we have lost the sense of the earth as a living being, as our Mother, and have come to view the world instead as a vast machine, a system of dead particles moved by external forces. The ecological and environmental crisis that begins to haunt us today (the pollution of our rivers, the destruction of the world's forests, acid rain, etc.) are a direct result of this way of thinking.

In modern medical science we witness the strange exercises of replacing human hearts with baboons' hearts (or mechanical hearts) and the growing experimentation with human embryos. It seems as though what is technically possible and progressive has become an end in itself without real consideration of the human consequences. We have pushed back the mysteries of life and death, making them legal rational concerns. In order to transplant organs, we have had to fix the moment of death into law; to experiment on embryos, we need to legalise the moment of life's beginning. Doctors now must decide whom to keep alive and whom to let die, who deserves a kidney machine and who does not. How can they decide? Today we begin to have the power to control and manipulate the forces of life and death. Yet, what are we to do with this power unless we learn to look at the questions of life and death in a new way. We need to find a new conception of life, a renewed imagination of the human being that can live in our daily thoughts and deeds and carry us into the future.

What is our conception of life today? What images do we live by? We have moved so far into abstraction and have so cut ourselves off from the rhythms of nature and the cosmos, from any sense of the renewing and sustaining energy of the spirit, that we are tempted to believe that we are merely very elaborate computers, machines with replaceable parts to be programmed at will. Valuing what we can see, measure and possess, it is hard for us to imagine that we are more than our physical, material bodies. We are taught about machines and how they work, but we are not taught about the human soul. And in the face of our mechanical models of the universe and the human being, in the face of denial and doubt, the human soul experiences desolation and meaninglessness.

Not only do we distrust our inner nature, but we all experience the lack of unity in this inner world of thoughts, feelings and impulses for actions. We often act from an abstract theory, although our hearts may prompt us to do something else. We can all think one thing, feel something different, and do something entirely out of harmony with both. We may be proud of our ability to think clearly, to articulate and to initiate, but we are often less sure or even apologetic about our softer, caring, nurturing sides, our more emotional, imaginative, intuitive capacities.

We are taught that our hearts, our inner lives, are not relevant to science or to the external world. We think that our fantasy life, together with myth and fairy tale, belong to childhood and are things we grow out of. That stones and flowers, rivers and even our household things have 'being' or presence, is 'mad', 'childish'. When, at two-and-a-half, my daughter told me with awe and conviction that her newly born sister had come from the lady moon, I was criticised for not correcting her and telling her the 'truth' – as though her picture did not contain the 'facts of life'. We are interested in behaviour but ashamed of feeling. We dismiss much of our experience by calling it sentimental. As the American poet Robert Duncan says in his book *The Truth and Life of Myth:*

"The modern mind has not only chickened out on the common things of our actual world, taking the properties of things as their uses and retracting all sense of fellow creatureliness. Not only the presences of gods and of ideas are denied, becoming for the modern man 'supposed' experiences, but the presence of stones, trees, animals and even men as spiritual beings is exorcised in our contemporary common sense. Where ever this contempt moves, it strikes to constrict the realm of empathy."[1]

Not only are we cut off from nature and from various aspects of ourselves but we are also isolated from one another. We are locked in ourselves, surrounded by relationships, yet alone; longing for friendships yet unable to sustain ongoing commitments, unable to move out of ourselves and get to know and trust one another. The divorce rate grows and family life becomes more difficult to sustain. People no longer feel they can count on their immediate family for love, care and support. Children and parents, brothers and sisters, do not necessarily understand each other. We have questioned the old roles and can no longer rely on the security and stability that they gave to our relationships in the past. More and more we meet as individuals without rules or roles, without any instinctive understanding to bring us together. Our growing consciousness of self turns quickly to a preoccupation with the individual personality and to excessive competition, manipulation and exploitation. In place of the social bonds that united people in the past anti-social forces foster independence and self-reliance. The number of people living alone is rising. Today many women and men choose to remain single; they do not want to become involved in or encumbered by a relationship. Without ties and the complexity of commitment, they feel they can be more independent, successful and productive. But our fear of losing our independence can truly imprison us, and without relationships with others we cannot begin to know and develop ourselves.

Through this experience of separation, however, we begin to wake up and search for ways to renew our interest in each other and our links with the earth and the spirit. Without rejecting what we have gained in knowledge, clarity and objectivity, we are now challenged to develop a consciousness that can lead us to wholeness, to a fuller understanding of life and the human being.

Seeds for this new understanding can be found everywhere, scattered amongst the darkness and difficulties of our time. Through the breakdown of traditional family life, people have found a greater freedom to establish new forms and ways of living together, not in relation to some fixed ideal but according to their individual capacities and needs. In different ways and circumstances, the old concept of family as relationships of blood is gradually being extended to include relationships of choice, based not on physical ties but on what flows between human hearts. As the destruction and waste of our natural world has become glaringly obvious, many people have begun to want to know the earth as a living being, our all-nourishing Mother, and to offer her their devoted care and respect. Also, while the developments in science and technology in our time stem from and foster a mechanistic view of life, they begin to point us beyond the physical sense-based reality. A growing number of people brought back to life by the ingenuity of medical science speak of their experience in a body-free state. Their stories validate the reality of the human spirit and remind us that we are more than our material bodies, that death is not an end but a new beginning, another kind of birth. The detailed knowledge of birth and embryological development that modern science has gathered has awakened in many people a sense of awe and wonder at the mystery of human life. Also in many fields of science, the threshold between the observer and that which is observed has begun to thin as more scientists become aware that what we are and think and feel affects the reality that we see and the discoveries that we make.

The breakdown of old thresholds or barriers, the meeting of what was hidden or inaccessible is part of a general awakening in our time. We want to look inward beyond our physical nature and outer personality to our more hidden qualities in order to bring them to expression and harmony; we want to know and express the divine within ourselves which is beyond all outer definitions. We also want to cross the threshold that separates us from one another, to meet the essential individuality of the other, free from the old stereotypes and expectations. And we search for meaning, for an inwardness in ourselves and in the world in response to the coldness, abstraction, and materialisation of modern life. We long to re-ensoul the world, and reawaken and explore the life of the soul within. This search is a manifestation of what Rudolf Steiner calls the crossing of the threshold, the thinning of the veil that for thousands of years cut people off from an experience of the spirit. Since the end of the last century, this veil has begun to lift and consciously or unconsciously we begin to search again for a path towards enlivened and balanced consciousness.

In the story of Ariadne that Signe Schaefer tells in her chapter, Ariadne gives the hero Theseus a magic ball of thread, a 'clue', that enables him to find his way to the centre of the labyrinth, kill the Minotaur and find his way out again. It is this same thread of essential life, of living, imaginative thinking that we need to find and take hold of today. The thread of Ariadne, of the feminine being that we seek, begins to tug and pull at us and, if we take hold of it, it can lead us on the path of self-knowledge, to meaning, truth and the birth of a new understanding. It is the thread of enlivened, heart-warmed consciousness which, if we follow it, can bring our life on earth once again into connection with the stars. I think that it is this same thread that William Blake speaks of in the following passage from his book *Jerusalem*.

> "I give you the end of the golden string
> Only wind it into a ball,
> It will lead you in at Heaven's Gate
> Built in Jerusalem's Wall."[2]

The American poetess, Denise Levertov, also writes of this thread:

The Thread

"Something is very gently
invisibly, silently,
pulling at me – a thread
or net of threads
finer than cobwebs and as
elastic. I haven't tried
the strength of it. No barbed hook
pierced and tore me. Was it
not long ago this thread
began to draw me? Or
way back? Was I
born with its knot about my
neck, a bridle? Not fear
but a stirring
of wonder makes me
catch my breath when I feel
the tug of it when I thought
it had loosened itself and gone."[3]

In this century the Feminist Movement has been one of the major forces to challenge the old order of things and to call us to cross the threshold to new levels of awareness. It has been part of the battle for the recognition of the human soul and a search for an equality of soul, for an understanding of the uniting force of our humanity which makes us truly brothers and sisters. It has also been a major stimulus to the awakening of new imagination of the feminine. It is true that women's initial struggle to win a greater dignity and consciousness, to ensure their right to self-determination and a voice in the world, sometimes clouded this purpose; often the feminine quality in women and its value in the world was hidden or even undermined and denied. Still today women neglect or forget their true source and aims. Yet there have begun to be changes and the deeper-lying aims of the Women's Movement have begun to surface.

Two years ago a student asked me: "Where is the Women's Movement today? In the 1960s women pushed for equal opportunities through political action in order to be equal with men. In the 1970s we thought we were better than men! You could look around and find a lot of strong women. But now, in the 1980s, where is the Movement? Nothing seems to be happening. Have women retreated?"

I think that what appeared to this woman as a retreat was and is an inward looking, a deepening of questions in the Movement today. Women have grown tired of a purely material analysis of their problems and seek to understand the more spiritual dimensions of their struggle for liberation; they want to discover what really is trying to be born out of the political and legal changes, out of women's awakening today; they are wanting to be true to their spiritual longings and to connect those deeper promptings and intuitions to responsible activity in the world. It is not hard though, to see why this in-turning might be called a retreat – it is quieter and less visible, and we generally feel uneasy about connecting our personal inner life with political questions and outer work. But as women set out on this quest for a soul, without going into retreat, they begin to pick up their true task – to help all of humanity to refind its soul.

Betty Friedan's book *The Second Stage*, which points to and calls for real changes in the Women's Movement, supports this view. Looking at the achievements, failures and responsibilities of the Movement, she calls for women and men to join together, free from the old limits and roles (and still without new or clear images of marriage, relationships, family life or work) and work for a new mobility and wholeness of soul for themselves and society, for a new meaning and understanding of life. She says that it is time for women to move beyond sexual politics, to renew and develop their capacity for warmth, sensitivity, flexibility and nurturing in the face of the increasing abstraction and materialisation of life and the forces of reaction and fear that would enslave us in the old ways and values. She says that the 'Second Stage' of the Movement, if it is to be a force for real social change, needs to pay more attention to family life, to the choice to have children, to new forms of community, new possibilities of work, and to other vital concerns of life.

This is quite clearly what more women are beginning to do as they turn their energy to concerns such as peace and ecology. And their activity has begun to bring changes. The women's peace camp at Greenham Common, the Cruise missile base at Newbury in England, is a continuing example and inspiration for the peace movement throughout the world. The women living there are not just protesting the deployment of Cruise missiles, or even the threat of nuclear war. Rather they have made it clear that they think peace is a much wider question connected with a whole way of life, with our values and attitudes towards life, and with issues of health, education, money, ecology, etc. Thus the Greenham women have done much to broaden the peace question, furthering an image of peace not just as an end product but as a path, a way of living responsibly and respectfully with others and the earth. Because of this, many more women have become involved in peace issues than otherwise would have done so, and the Women's Movement itself has found a broader base.

It has also been important how women have worked, not just what they have worked at. They have worked together without hierarchy or leaders, everyone sharing responsibility. They have sought new ways of protesting from the reactive, militant, slogan-chanting ways of the 1960s. Working with symbol, art and song, planting flowers, lighting candles, women have found loving, imaginative ways to affirm life and creation in the face of death and destruction. In this new work women seem to be offering as a gift to the world what they have developed and gained through household work, as they have cared for and nurtured the imaginative, feeling life of the small circle of their homes. This invisible and quiet work of centuries now begins to flow out into the larger world as a source of strength and inspiration for us all, as an offering for the whole of humanity for the continuation of life on earth.

It has seemed to me that at Greenham Common, however ugly and difficult it may appear, women are somehow recognising and serving the new feminine, the new Mary, which wants to be born on earth in our time. The picture of women holding hands and encircling the missile base with love and the details of their lives (toys, children's clothing, photographs, flowers, ribbons, candle light) is a picture of hope and life meeting and standing firm in the face of death and despair. It calls to mind the image in 'The Revelation of St. John the Divine' of the woman who is "clothed with the sun, and the moon under her feet, and upon her head a crown of twelve stars",[4] who gives birth to a child and is threatened by a dragon. The serpent in 'Revelations' is banished to the earth. It is, I think, the same serpent that women at Greenham now embrace and meet with a courage and responsibility towards life.

At Greenham the feminine struggling to be born today grows visible, particularly in her aspect as the Mother of Peace and the Mother of the Earth. In the New Testament, she is called Mary. To find Mary today, to become 'a Mary' means to step onto a path of development that leads to the awakening of the heart's vision; it means to 'go in peace'. The women at Greenham Common may be far away from such a goal and yet, however imperfectly, they have begun to listen to and recover something of the feminine which is central to our need to find a warmth that can penetrate the extreme coldness and rationality around us. In service of the Mother of Peace and the Being of the earth, women have now begun to take up their task as guardians of life and peace on earth. A friend wrote a poem about her experience of Mary at the Greenham camp which I would like to include here, as it captures something of the search that many people are engaged in for this new feminine, for the voice of the New Mary:

> If in time to come
> a child should ask me Why? . . . How?
> I would reply
> there came upon the Earth a New Mary . . .
> She sung songs
> She built a web
> She grew like a great flower in the light of
> her own truth and sisterhood
> She was the Mary of Joys and Sorrows
> She was the inward meeting of the rivers

She was the moon and tides of ocean and blood
She was the wound . . . and she was wise.
I met her while I danced
And when I heard the wolf howling in my soul
and saw its silent agony behind another's eyes
      she was with me . . .
I found my tears upon her face
And it was the face of the living God . . .
I found her weeping in the holocaust
searching for the million children she had lost
I heard her scream as she looked upon their faces
      I was with her . . .
I found my strength with her –
standing silent by the wire
And as I struggled with my anger and my fear
She told me that we are the weavers
      of the New day
She held me . . . this New Mary
"We are the purpose" she said
"The vision is us".[5]

This is I think a 'modern' imagination of Mary, relevant to our time. Can we find other pictures of her living today? What is this new transformed feminine that we seek? What is our relationship to her? What does she mean to us? The feminine as Madonna is one of the oldest images we know. We can follow her development and transformation from early stone figures dated from 19,000 BC, through her many faces from all over the world as Great Mother and Great Goddess, to her various representations today, in modern literature and art or in the faces, gestures, work and purposes of the women at Greenham. The Feminist Movement, through its general consciousness raising and historical studies, has encouraged and has been particularly responsible for awakening an imagination of the feminine in the last 20 years. It has made us aware that she is not only part of our heritage and our humanity but has much to do with our present and future. This came home to me several years ago when I read about a feminist group in Russia called the Maria Club, who met together to explore the meaning of Mary to them. They wanted Russian women to look again at what was called freedom and equality, women in hard labour with their children in day care and feminine values undermined. These women said that their primary aim was to work for the recognition of the individual human soul in the face of the abstraction and dehumanisation of our lives.

This is one place where women are working to find a living and modern relation to the feminine. But parts of the Women's Movement also seem to look backwards, fostering a kind of revival of goddess worship and rituals of communion with Mother Earth. This makes me uneasy, for I do not think we want to resurrect from the past the old instinctive feminine. Nor do we want just another abstraction. The feminine that we search for today needs to have gone through the eye of the needle of our modern, individual, analytic consciousness. She arises out of the breakdown of the old order; she stands at the edge of the abyss, and, if we seek her, she will open the way for our new development and a new flowering of our humanity, for she calls us to renew ourselves and the imagination.

In a lecture series called *The Search for the New Isis, Divine Sophia,*[6] given in 1920, Rudolf Steiner calls on humanity to set out in search of the New Isis, the force which enables us to see through the outer world of the senses to the inwardness and moral meaning of the world. With the development of the mechanical, abstract world view where the stars move according to mechanical necessity, this spiritual essence of the world, the divine wisdom or Sophia of the universe, was lost. To re-ensoul the world, to develop true insight and understanding into the universe and the human being, we need to create new living imaginations of the Isis, the Mother of the World, the Queen of Heaven and the Earth – imaginations not of the past but appropriate to our time. Steiner says that the new Isis, the Isis of the New Age, is a veiled being sleeping within humanity and that it is our task today to lift her veil. She is not just a frozen archetype outside of us, but a living capacity sleeping within everyone of us, waiting to be reawakened.

Although there are many levels and meanings connected with Steiner's call to us to find anew this Mary being of the world, I think the Women's Movement is one place today where we can find this search going on. The vision of 'the lady' can also be found living in the poems of many modern poets. In the poetry of the American poetess Hilda Doolittle (H.D.) 'the lady' appears as a living being who signals the emergence of new creative capacities in human beings. In the poem *Tribute to the Angels,* after picturing how the lady has been seen the world over in so many different faces and forms,

H.D. describes Her as She appeared to her, carrying a book which was however not filled with all the ancient wisdom but rather was a book of the "unwritten volume of the new".

". . . she is not shut up in a cave
like a Sibyl; she is not

imprisoned in leaden bars
in a coloured window;

she is Psyche, the butterfly,
out of the cocoon.

But nearer than Guardian Angel
or good Daemon,

she is the counter-coin-side
of primitive terror;

she is not-fear, she is not-war,
but she is no symbolic figure

of peace, charity, chastity, goodness,
faith, hope, reward;

she is not Justice with eyes
blindfolded like Love's;

I grant you the dove's symbolic purity,
I grant you her face was innocent

and immaculate and her veils
like the Lamb's Bride,

but the Lamb was not with her,
either as Bridegroom or Child;

her attention is undivided,
we are her bridegroom and lamb;

her book is our book; . . ."[7]

Polarity and Balance

If we want to find this feminine being in the world and in ourselves and thereby come to a fuller picture of who we are, then it is important not to ignore or diminish the masculine qualities that are also a part of this picture. Masculine and feminine are two sides of one polarity; they belong together and cannot be known without each other.

In her chapter, Signe Schaefer traces the interweaving of feminine and masculine forces through prehistory and history, looking at the meaning (for evolution) of our incarnation into polarity. She suggests that it is through the interplay and struggle between these two forces and through the growth of the masculine influence and the waning of the feminine, that our individual self-consciousness developed. She makes it clear that the development of the masculine in both women and men in the whole of western society has been important and necessary. It has made possible the growth of individuality, the capacity for objectivity and clarity of thought, and for free scientific enquiry; it has allowed for the emergence of individual responsibility and, therefore, for heroism, morality, relationship and love. However, today this masculine development has become extreme and one-sided so that together with its positive manifestations we increasingly find its negative – the depersonalization, isolation and alienation of modern life; the blind search for personal power and possessions; the science of war and the manipulation of life; the neglect of the heart life. Without the balancing force of the feminine, the masculine has become narrow-visioned and destructive, cutting us off from ourselves, from each other, the earth and the spiritual in the universe.

Caught in this one-sided development, trapped in materialism, a longing for the spirit and a desire to understand and include the life of the soul began to grow in people in this century. We have seen that the Feminist Movement arose as part of this search. And working through its many faces and aspects has been the fundamental aim to bring a new warmth and balance, a new relationship between feminine and masculine qualities, by a revaluing and a new recognition of women and also the feminine qualities which they carry and serve. The true aims of the Movement have not been to replace men with women or the masculine with the feminine, but to warm and ensoul the masculine, to bring the feminine, imaginative, healing, nurturing qualities together with the masculine clarity, objectivity

and individuality. With an enlivened feminine we can begin to warm
our frozen consciousness, enliven our feeling life and refind our
connection with the spirit. We can find ways to bring a more
peripheral awareness of the whole together with our absolute straight
truths, to bring knowledge together with life, heart into what we think
and do. Then the vast amount of knowledge that we have gathered can
become a window to the spiritual reality that weaves behind our
material existence. Then we can know our connections to each other
and the world, and can begin to build a new life consciousness and a
new understanding of human life on earth.

In order to work towards this ideal of balance, we need to value both
the feminine and masculine, and to know them in their positive and
negative manifestations. Then we can work to find the force within us
that can control and direct these qualities and bring them into a more
conscious and creative interaction.

In characterising feminine and masculine it is increasingly
important to be clear about the shifting and interweaving levels of the
polarity, and especially to recognise the distinction between the
polarity of woman/man and feminine/masculine. This understanding
is growing today. As people look within themselves they realise that
whether they are women or men, they all have both feminine and
masculine qualities. Although women embody the feminine and men
embody the masculine and therefore have a more direct, primary
relationship to that quality, these qualities are not tied exclusively to
either sex. Rather, they are two archetypal energies ever at work in all
individuals, all relationships and in society as a whole, central forces
in the evolution of human consciousness and in the development and
expression of the human spirit. Although in individuals and in society
these forces are often out of balance and in conflict, today we can and
must begin to find the inner force of soul that can bring them into a
dynamic union, a union which is at once a movement and a stillness,
which is an inner peace. To awaken to and to acknowledge this source,
the free spirit that works within both women and men, has been a
fundamental work of women in this century. They have called us to
look behind the male or female garment that we wear and to recognise
our essential individuality, that which is independent of our particular
sex and upon which we can base our true equality. It is this
individuality, or ego, which increasingly determines our path in life
and which can begin to integrate and balance the different qualities of
feminine and masculine within our souls.

So I want to characterise the feminine and masculine, but these qualities and pictures should not be directly applied to women or men. It is also important not to fix these definitions too rigidly. The feminine-masculine polarity is one of the fundamental mysteries of human existence, and therefore, in trying to understand it, we must work with and tolerate paradox. The polarity will not hold still. Saying one thing, it is often possible to say the opposite. The feminine that women express outwardly is somehow different from the feminine that works in the soul of a man. It is difficult to take hold of the subtlety of this polarity, but it is important to know that it is subtle. Otherwise, instead of working creatively towards a harmony, we will once again find ourselves stuck in old or new stereotypes.

The Feminine

The gesture of the feminine pole is that of a round, a circle, a vessel, encompassing, unifying, synthesising, transforming, nurturing. Feminine consciousness is a diffuse, peripheral consciousness that does not come to something directly but from various points on the periphery. It is our capacity to see and carry the whole. The feminine is open and vulnerable, intuitive and rhythmic; it trusts, accepts, waits, and listens; it is connected with the life of feeling and the imagination.

These qualities, like the masculine qualities which I will characterise later, have their negative pole. Waiting can be active, but it can also be static, a kind of vegetating. Protecting, caring, embracing can become extreme, and manifest as smothering or ensnaring. Similarly, diffuseness can be vague, softness can be weakness. The feminine can be flexible or scatty, imaginative or fantastic, rich feeling or chaotic, undisciplined emotion. The feminine round can be receptive, open and patient, but we can also fall asleep within it and lose touch with the outside world. The intimacy and warmth of the feminine can become stifling and posssessive. I have experienced that sometimes, sitting round the table with my two daughters when my husband comes home. Sometimes we are laughing and playing and making a ring that excludes him, making him feel a stranger in an alien world. Marie Louise van Franz looks at the fairytale *Snow White and Rose Red* from this perspective.[8] She speaks of how the beginning of the tale creates a mood of harmony, balance and perfection; the two girls and their mother with the lamb and the dove, sitting around the hearth, evoke a sense of Paradise before the Fall. All is goodness, purity and innocence. But it is also a static world until a bear, the masculine element, enters the scene. He brings movement and adventure, a breadth, scope and objectivity.

The feminine round stands at the beginning of time; it is our mother's womb and the collective world womb in which all humanity began, where all was eternal and divine, where all opposites embraced each other and all potentials existed unrealised. The mother's womb is also a veil, behind which, concealed from the senses, the new human being develops.

Paradise in the Bible is often pictured as a womb within which Adam and Eve live in innocence and eternity before the Fall. They are not yet earthly man and woman but together they represent the whole human being, still partaking of the celestial and archetypal nature of Adam in the first chapter of Genesis.

The ancient Egyptian symbol of the uroboros (the circular serpent biting its own tail) also represents an unconscious feminine oneness of all, the beginning of all things, when day and night, inner and outer, heaven and earth, male and female, were one. "It slays, weds and impregnates itself. It is man and woman begetting and conceiving, devouring and giving birth, active and passive, above and below, at one."[9]

In their beginnings, all human beings participate in this feminine round. In his *Symposium* Plato describes the original androgynous human beings as round. Rudolf Steiner also speaks of the ancient human form as round, egg-like and fluid. He says that originally human beings were unisexual, both female and male in one and yet, in their physical form, were somehow more female-like. They were chalices, receiving and being fertilised by the spiritual rays of wisdom.

The feminine is the unconscious round of our beginnings and it also initiates the recovery of that wholeness in consciousness. It is the renewed vision of the heart, the cosmic wisdom of the Divine Sophia, the New Jerusalem, who will re-ensoul the earth and humanity. In his book *The Divine Adventure*, Fiona Macleod speaks of the important role to be played by this feminine being in our future, when he remembers an old Celtic Christian prophecy that Christ will come again in the form of a woman:

"I believe that we are close upon a great and deep spiritual change. I believe a new redemption is even now conceived of the Divine Spirit in the human heart, that is itself as a woman, broken in dreams, and yet sustained in faith, patient, long-suffering, looking towards home. I believe that though the Reign of Peace may be yet a long way off, it is drawing near; and that who shall save us anew shall come divinely as a Woman, to save as Christ saved, but not, as He did, to bring with Her a sword. But whether this Divine Woman, this Mary of so many passionate hopes and dreams, is to come through mortal birth, or as an immortal Breathing upon our souls, none can yet know."

"Sometimes I dream of the old prophecy that Christ shall come again upon Iona, and of that later and obscure prophecy which foretells, now as the Bride of Christ, now as the Daughter of God, now as the Divine Spirit embodied through mortal birth in a woman, as once through mortal birth as a Man, the coming of a new Presence and Power: and dream that this may be upon Iona, so that the little Gaelic island may become as the little Syrian Bethlehem. But more wise it is to dream, not of hallowed ground, but the hallowed gardens of the soul wherein She shall appear white and radiant. Or that, upon the hills, where we are wandered, the Shepherdess shall call us home."[10]

The eternal Feminine embodied in Mary, or in her various appearances and transformations throughout history as Great Goddess, as the Mother Soul of the World, points to several different aspects of the feminine.

The feminine is a principle of oneness and unity. The ancient goddess, representing the wholeness of all life, was often a virgin moon goddess. She was complete in herself; having both feminine and masculine principles within, she did not need any outside complement. She represented the unified, primeval wisdom of all and recalled a time when all humanity was open to the spiritual essence of life.

Moon goddesses ruled the earth when a more dream-like, night-time, feminine consciousness prevailed, when what was experienced in sleep and dream was clearer and more real than the things of the daytime world. Rudolf Steiner speaks of this time in the distant past and says that during this time people were open to the instreaming of divine wisdom and had direct perception of the creative forces working behind and within the things of the world. Night was the time of birth and day the time of death. Gradually in the course of human development this clairvoyant consciousness faded. The night time world dimmed for people and the daylight, sense-perceptible world came into sharper focus. Today our waking sense-based consciousness predominates; sleep and dream are sometimes even regarded as empty, wasted hours. Any feeling or vision is seen as personal and subjective, and therefore unreal. Perhaps now, in reawakening the feminine, we need to "open Night's eye that sleeps in what we know by day",[11] and so come to a conscious and individual knowledge of the essence of life.

The feminine is connected with rhythm, an awareness of the flow and fluidity, the ever-changing oneness of all. During the rule of the Great Goddesses, people felt united with the world and each other, and knew themselves as part of the folk and community rather than as separate individuals. The Great Goddess embodied the eternal cycle of existence and the unity of all life. She was the regulator of fertility, the ruler of the stars and the earth, the waxing and waning moon, the birth, life, death and resurrection of nature. She was at once the Queen of Heaven and the Mother of the Earth, the spirit moving behind the stars and the fertile earth that brings forth the golden sheaths of corn each harvest time.

People were still in touch with this feminine being in the Middle Ages. They knew her as Natura, the goddess of Nature, the life giver, healer, the inward sphere of the earth. She was represented as a beautiful goddess, crowned with the signs of the Zodiac and the planets and clothed with robe, mantle, tunic, undergarments and shoes on which were depicted the whole of the created universe, all the many varied forms of nature, from the creatures of the air, earth and water to the herbs, trees and flowers of the earth. People knew this feminine being, this Mother Earth, also as Mary, Mother of God, mediator between heaven and earth, the heart wisdom of the Holy Spirit, the all nourishing, protecting, healing Mother of the World. Emil Bock speaks of this connection between the healing goddess of nature and the Virgin Mary in the following passage:

"There are many places the Virgin Mary is said to have performed, and where sanctuaries of Mary were set up. One can now recognise that all such places are places which have an especial etheric character which is usually externalised in a spring. This came to me with special force on the slopes of the Odilienberg in Alsace, in S. Maria del Sasso near Locarno, and at a Spring, sacred to Mary, upon Mount Athos. Such places were already known and held sacred in pre-Christian times. The Odilienberg, indeed, was the place of a Celtic Druidical sanctuary. It may have been at such places that one met through vision, or through feeling, the great 'goddess Nature', the life giver. Visions and acts of healing in which, in earlier times, one met Diana or the goddess Nature, were transferred in Christian times to the Virgin Mary. There are in the etheric world, which surrounds and penetrates our earth, etheric centres where something of the inward sphere, of the hidden Mother Soul of the cosmos wells forth. At such places the harmonising, health-giving, healing action which must in earlier times have proceeded forth from nature more strongly than now, reveals itself in a concentrated way: at such places it is as if the earth had preserved something of the paradisal innocence and purity which it possessed before the Fall."[12]

The feminine then, found in its purity and strength in Mary, is an awareness of the relationship of microcosm to macrocosm, of the human being to earth and stars, of the inwardness of the human being to the outwardness of the world. We can find this awareness today in the growing interest in holistic medicine where the aim is to heal and harmonise the whole person and to engage the will of the individual in his or her own healing process rather than to treat only the physical manifestation of the illness. A new feminine impulse also works behind the growing hospice movement, which tries to provide places where both the physical and soul needs of dying people can be met. Ideally the whole environment in a hospice becomes a protecting, caring vessel in which the patient can rest. The growing consciousness and interest in death and dying in recent years, reflected in the work of Elizabeth Kübler-Ross or in such a book as *Life After Life* by Raymond Moody, also signifies a renewed feminine awareness of the rhythms and cycles of existence; we are gradually remembering that death is not only an ending but a birth and a new beginning.

Mary as Divine Sophia also embodies the feminine as inspirational wisdom, as creative understanding through which we can connect ourselves to our origins and can rediscover what is deepest in humanity, a knowing which allows us to see through and understand the external world. She is the Muse through whom we find the creative source of the world. She guides us across the inner and outer threshold.

Feminine thinking is imaginative and intuitive; it knows the presences and the inner gestures of things and their interconnections; it grasps the living wholeness of the world. The feminine does not divide spirit from matter, mind from body, ideas from life. The feminine is sensitive to atmosphere, tone and mood; it is aware of what lives in the silences and spaces between people and things, of what is not said as well as what is said, of who a person is as well as what they do. The feminine is the principle that brings us into relationships; it wants to merge and be one with, to co-operate and share.

In its new awakening today, the feminine stirs in the self-conscious individual new social forces, new interest in others; it stimulates us to live and work together with others. For now when we have gained independence and strength of self, we can begin to truly give to each other and find the possibility of a conscious and selfless love.

The feminine is a vessel for re-birth and transformation. It is the chalice, the baptismal font, the hearth, the philosopher's egg (the alchemical vessel in which base metal was transformed into gold). It is Noah's Ark, which is a moon boat in which humanity and all "wherein is the breath of life" co-mingle and ride the flood waters into a new birth. The story of the flood in the Bible is a creation story in which female and male are united and made whole before the birth of a new humanity.

The feminine in myth and history has often worked as an evolutionary force transforming the human spirit. Eve, in listening to the serpent and eating of the fruit of the Tree of Knowledge, takes the first step towards independent consciousness and freedom. In the very early epochs of human development on earth, what Rudolf Steiner calls "a pre-eminence of the feminine soul"[13] was responsible for the first progress in communal life, the first development of the life of imagination, the formation of memory, customs and morals. Archaeological findings and modern feminist research conclude with Steiner that, in this early time of humanity's beginnings, it was through women that religion, language, song and poetry developed.

The transforming activity of the feminine can also be seen in what were traditionally 'women's tasks' – weaving, potting, farming, cooking and mothering. In past matriarchal societies, these activities were sacred because they were concerned with the essential mysteries of life; they were to do with the transformation of the material to the spiritual. Many of these activities took place around the hearth, which was also an altar, a sacred social centre. Places of birth were also temples. Birth was a primary mystery, and in giving birth women achieved a transformation of their own nature and made themselves vessels for the working together of spirit and matter.

The Madonna is the archetypal feminine as mother. She is the chalice, open and receiving, overflowing with love and understanding; she nurtures, protects, sustains, and maintains. She is strong in her acceptance of life and her capacity to serve. Knowing that there is time, that all things grow and ripen through time, she creates a silence and a stillness, a space for things to mature and become what they truly are. She allows us to make ourselves vulnerable, to reveal ourselves with our weaknesses and strengths. She is patient and tolerant, allowing, accepting and trusting. Coming to her in distress, she gives us peace. She is the pure, receptive soul which can give birth to what is highest in humanity. She is the vessel in which love can be born.

The feminine, in the image of Mary the mother of Jesus, is a picture of innocence and devotion, the listening, still, yet inwardly active receptivity of the heart. In Luke's Gospel in the Bible, Mary responds to the events of her son's life by keeping and pondering those events "in her heart". By this activity Mary is shown to us as the archetype of the meditating soul, receiving the words spoken to her, keeping and protecting them, and allowing them to ripen. Emil Bock says that "as Mary receives the words of the angels, the words told by the shepherds, and the words of the 12-year-old Jesus in her heart, with meditative thought, she lets their spiritual meaning emerge from them like spiritual forms. In the soul of Mary there emerges from each group of words, a spiritual butterfly."[14]

The feminine, as pure and open heart, listens to the inwardness of the world. She listens across the threshold of the other, into the true intention of the other, into the inwardness of their being. She listens to the unborn, to what is wanting to be born, and in listening she helps what is unborn come to birth so that the other can become what they long to be. She empties herself in order to be filled by the true concept of the other, by the divinity that lives within the other.

This kind of listening is part of the path of development described by Rudolf Steiner in his book *Knowledge of the Higher Worlds and its Attainment*. In this book Steiner gives an exercise through which we can work to develop our capacity to listen with our soul. He describes how we have to practise listening in such a way that our inner self is stilled. All assent or dissent, all intellectual judgment as well as all feelings of sympathy and antipathy, all our prejudices and feelings of self, must be let go. "The student can thus train himself to listen to the words of others quite selflessly, completely shutting out his own person, and his opinions and way of feeling. When he practises listening without criticism, even when a completely contradictory opinion is advanced, when the 'hopeless mistake' is committed before him, then he learns, little by little, to blend himself with the being of another and become identified with it. Then he hears through the words, into the soul of the other."[15]

To me, the archetypal picture of this kind of listening is found in the description that Rudolf Steiner gives of the conversation between Jesus and his mother before the baptism in the Jordan where, Steiner says, the being of Jesus received the Christ.[16] Jesus comes to speak to his mother in crisis, full of distress at the state of humanity. Her deep and still listening allows him to unburden his soul. It allows him to empty himself and makes possible the next step in his great destiny. Through Mary's power of listening, he is able to realize his deepest purpose and to receive the Christ, his higher being. According to Steiner, by taking on herself the burdens of her son and of humanity, Mary also experiences a transformation of her being at this moment. She becomes the incarnation of the Divine Sophia, the divine mother and wisdom of all.

So this is a picture of Mary, of the feminine, as the birthplace of understanding. The questions for us are: Can we find Mary within? Can we develop this power of listening that allows another person to find their next step? Can we become the birthplace of understanding for someone else, and thereby help them along? Can we learn to carry in our hearts the destinies of others? Mary is the picture of the soul which develops compassionate understanding of another person's destiny, or of our time and the destiny of humanity; she holds a picture of what one human being, or what the whole of humanity can become. Mary is that within us which can conceive a new imagination of the human being.

Perhaps this capacity for listening is rare, but if we have ever even for a moment experienced it, either through our own inner efforts or through grace, we never lose the love and faith in the being of the other that we meet at that moment. We always carry the secret of their being within us. I think we witness people working for a re-emergence and development of this feminine capacity in the many attempts since the 1960s to form new communities, not out of blood but out of what flows between human hearts. People search today to find new ways to work together and to attend to their relationships, to come through the loneliness of the birth of self and begin to meet and give to each other out of their self. We long to meet beyond our sympathies and antipathies, our likes and dislikes, our prejudices and opinions, beyond our nation, race, sex, or family, and to find and recognise the true being within the other. This kind of knowing of the other requires that we become inwardly active. It requires an inner soul-work. We have to wake up in our meetings and bring to them a consciousness, an activity of will, and most of all a heart warmth, a warmth of true interest in the other. And this means a reawakening of the feminine, of the heart's power of listening.

The Masculine

While the ear, receiving, listening and balancing is a feminine organ, throughout time the eye has been a symbol for the masculine, for clear perception, objective, focussed thinking. We say, "I see" when we suddenly understand something which the moment before was cloudy and unclear. The eye stands for awakening and the light of consciousness. When we want to meet someone consciously we look them directly in the eyes. Something of the essence or individuality of a person is revealed in their eyes. If someone is "out of themselves", absent in consciousness, not quite awake, their gaze may be blank, glazed and distant. A relationship then exists between I and eye, between eye sight and our sense of ourselves as independent ego beings. When our eyes focus a duality becomes a unity. Through this activity consciousness arises.

If the original unconscious round of existence is feminine, the division of that primeval unity and the fall into opposites is masculine. In many myths the original feminine oneness is divided, light is released and the world becomes manifest. What was indefinite and unformed, has become definite, formed and visible. Time, space and boundaries are created. In the pre-Hellenic creation myth, Eurynome, the Goddess of All Things, rises naked from chaos but finding nothing substantial for her feet to rest upon she divides the sea from the sky, and dances lonely on the waves before creation. She calls the masculine principle, the great serpent Ophion, into existence. Then she becomes a dove brooding on the waters, and eventually lays the universal cosmic egg. She commands Ophion to coil around it seven times. In due course, the egg hatches and all the created world spills out of it. In the Babylonian "Enuma Elish", the sun hero, Marduk, battles with Tiamet, the mother of the gods, who has gradually become a demonical and destructive force. Marduk tears her in pieces and creates heaven and earth out of her body. This masculine gesture of dismembering or disremembering the divine wisdom and wholeness was necessary for creation to take place. It was also necessary for the development of human consciousness, for from this separation and division we gain the possiblity of knowledge of ourselves and of the world through which we can freely rediscover the divine and once more achieve harmony.

Paradise in the Bible depicts the original unconscious round, our primeval perfecion and wholeness, where all rests in eternity, in the bosom of the godhead. Adam and Eve in Paradise are still not earthly man and woman. Together they are the whole human being, existing in a state of divine union. But, when they eat of the Tree of Knowledge, they lose their wholeness and become man and woman. They are cast out of Paradise into the material world, but they also acquire a new independence. They become "as gods, knowing good and evil". "The eyes of them both were opened and they knew that they were naked". [17]

Adam and Eve experience the first flash of ego consciousness, the dawning of the capacity for thought, through which they can now strive towards self perfection and immortality. They acquire the ability to make distinctions. Light penetrates their inner darkness and the development of an inner life becomes possible. Adam and Eve cut themselves off from divine guidance and must begin to create a new law and order for themselves out of the power of their potential individuality.

The Genesis creation story points to a masculine path of development. A new knowledge had to be gathered based on sense perception of the external world. Adam had to go out into the world and 'till the soil'. He had to work in the world and develop a new knowledge by distinguishing, observing and collecting the things of the material world. He had to evolve a thinking through which human beings could discover their individual relation to the spirit.

Our individual development follows this masculine path. We grow out of the round of early childhood and stand upright and say 'I'. We gradually distinguish between ourselves and the world. We learn the names of things, and the differences between them. The circle games of early childhood through which children enact their experience of the wholeness of life, are replaced by line games ("A hunting we will go", "Nuts in May", "Follow the leader") in which some independence and individual skill are required. Children become increasingly conscious of boundaries, rules, authority and polarity, and their feeling of individuality grows.

If the feminine gesture is round, the masculine gesture is that of a straight line, directing, penetrating, pursuing, perceiving. It distinguishes, defines, separates, analyses, individualises. It is precise, clear, firm and focussed, objective and rational, and is connected with the intellect and the will. The masculine is as valuable and necessary for life and creativity as the feminine. Both qualities belong together and need each other. Like the feminine, the masculine can move too far out of balance and become negative. Masculine clarity can be cold, directness can demolish, discipline can turn to violence. To separate can be to isolate, individuality can become selfish, objectivity can be detachment, and the intellect can become theoretical and dry, far removed from life. Similarly, to control can be to manipulate, to be focussed can be one-sided and oblivious of surroundings. To guide or discriminate may be to dominate or to be prejudiced, to judge may be to be judgmental, will can become brute force and a lust for power. I looked at some of the imbalances of the masculine in our time in detail earlier; we know well the destruction and unhappiness that an unbalanced masculine force can bring, but we must also remember its positive and continuing contribution to our individual lives and the life of the earth.

Without the masculine which divides there could be no individuality. Our self-conscious awareness, our sense of our uniqueness is masculine. Through it we gain independence and loneliness. Our masculine consciousness breaks the bonds that unite us with community, nature and the universe. It cuts us off from cosmic and earthly rhythms and from our own bodies. The impulse to know ourselves and to understand the world separates us from life. Standing alone, relying on ourselves, concerned with our development, we become isolated from others. Yet this separation can lead to true relationships. Love as a free gift, a selfless love, is only possible if we have a self to give. Only if we develop ourselves can we work inwardly to awaken a conscious and heartfelt interest in the other. So the masculine self consciousness ultimately makes possible freedom, social responsibility and love.

The growing masculine development which began to break through as a major force in human consciousness at the dawn of known history, can be characterised as a movement from a more feminine, imaginative night consciousness to a more intellectual, day consciousness. Rudolf Steiner describes the shift in awareness in the following passage:

"When he was awake man saw darkly what was physical, but as though it were wrapped in mist and surrounded by an aura of light. In his sleep man rose to the spiritual worlds and the divine spiritual beings. He alternated between a clairvoyant consciousness, which grew ever weaker, and a day consciousness, an object consciousness, which grew stronger and stronger and is the head consciousness of today. Gradually he lost the capacity of clairvoyant perception, together with the faculty for seeing the gods in sleep. However, the clarity of day consciousness waxed in the same proportion, and the consciousness of self, and "I" feeling, the "I" perception, grew stronger."[18]

This development was a gradual one. As the sense of ego grew, human beings slowly moved away from their more feminine cosmic consciousness and their sense of union with the world, out of a more mythic time into historical time and a growing awareness of the sense world. As the individual intellect began to emerge, people stepped onto a path of self-consciousness, self-determination and alienation. Individual thought and perception came to be valued and revelation and clairvoyance began to dim. William Irving Thompson in his excellent book *The Time Falling Bodies Take To Light* puts this shift at about 4000 to 3000 BC, the time of the growth of the Sumarian, Babylonian and Egyptian civilisations. This was the time of the movement "from Neolithic villages to organised states, from gardening to irrigation farming, from iconography to writing, from disorganised raids to institutional warfare, from custom to law, from matriarchal, religious authority to patriarchal, political power, from mystery to history."[19]

This masculine development which began to emerge in Sumaria and clearly announced itself in Greece and Rome, was also characterised by the growth of philosophy and science and by the striving to know the world through the intellect and will, by the development of clear, logical thinking, and by the emergence of the capacity to judge and evaluate. All of these faculties contributed to the development of the sense of self, to the growth of law and civilisation and to our ever increasing control over our lives. As the 'night-time' consciousness faded, the great mothers who ruled over the childhood of humanity lost their power to their sons, the emerging heroes who overthrew the old matriarchal order and founded new patriarchal states. These were the sun heroes who, with their individual skill and cunning, with their strength of character and steadfastness of will, battled the dragons and monsters of the old, dark order, and heralded a new age of light and reason, clarity and consciousness. They had to be watchful, wakeful, alert, they had to go through trials of staying awake in order to defeat their foes, gain the treasure, or win the princess. These qualities were specifically developed and tested in men's groups and secret societies in the past. The purpose of these ancient brotherhoods seems to have been to develop the higher masculine, to oppose the older feminine wisdom and eventually to capture its power.

In a variety of ways, their mysteries had to do with the birth of the ego and the initiation of the individual. In their initiations, as in many myths and fairy tales, the sun, the light, the eye and the head are symbols for evolving masculine consciousness.

Just as the eternal feminine qualities are contained in the image of the Sophia or Maria, the archetypal masculine is revealed through the nature and actions of the many heroes of myth and legend. One of the earliest stories of a hero filled with masculine striving and a sense of an awakening ego-consciousness is the Sumarian-Babylonian epic of Gilgamesh. In this story the masculine emerges as a ruling force challenging and finally displacing the feminine and the old connection with the cosmos. Gilgamesh is a new kind of hero, searching for knowledge, concerned with making his mark. He wants to make a name for himself, to have his name stamped on stone as a monument to his personality. Not content to live in the moment, he desires to influence the future. Gilgamesh is no longer one with the world of nature and the stars. Even his city is a walled city, contained, limited and cut off from its surroundings.

Although this is a loss, Gilgamesh embodies in its positive form the masculine force that has shaped our Western civilisation and the development of our individual consciousness. The masculine names, defines, categorises and limits. It seeks knowledge of the world through collecting and combining, studying, inspecting, dissecting and dividing the things of the world. It wants to know – what something is, how it works, what it means.

In Jean Paul Sartre's novel *Nausea*,[20] the figure of the Autodidact captures something of the masculine passion for collecting information and its way towards knowledge and erudition. The Autodidact is a lonely, highly organized and systematic scholar who teaches himself in alphabetical order. With unswerving determination, he sets out to read all the books in the library, beginning with 'A' and moving resolutely towards 'Z'. His path is logical, linear and apparently direct as opposed to the more round-about, intuitive feminine way based on the relationships between all things. The Autodidact formulates a plan and then works step-by-step towards the realization of his goal – to know everything.

The masculine orders and plans; it seeks power, fame, recognition and individual freedom. In contrast to the feminine which yields and lets go, the masculine masters, guides, and regulates; it is determined and resolute. The masculine wants to determine the future and know all the answers while the feminine accepts that there are not always reasonable answers for everything. The feminine knows how to wait and allow things to happen. It relinquishes control and understands that some things in life cannot be forced to happen. If the feminine is interested in process, the masculine looks for results and conclusions. Masculine thinking is logical and linear, conceptual and abstract; it deals with the external, material surface of things; it is interested in the tangible achievements of the intellect and the will, in what can be observed with the senses, measured, weighed, quantified, used. It always wants to know the main points, the skeleton, the bones of any proposal or idea. It organises, classifies, compartmentalises, specialises; it is concerned with authority, hierarchy, and individual initiative and ability.

The qualities of feminine and masculine have sometimes been seen in terms of left and right (dexterity, not politics). Traditionally, the left has been associated with the receptive, the intuitive, the artistic, the imaginative, the magical and with the moon, the night, the irrational. The right has been associated with the sun, the day, the rational, the active, the intellectual, and the powerful. It is likely that left-handedness predominated in our more matriarchal past, whereas today the majority of people are right-handed. This may be an expression of the fact that we primarily value the verbal, analytical and cognitive skills connected with the left side of the brain. It seems the right side of the brain (which corresponds to the left side of the body) is more connected to our interpretive, intuitive, artistic, musical abilities. These two spheres of the brain, however, do not function independently but are connected by an isthmus of nerve tissue called the corpus callosum which integrates the different kinds of learning within the brain. Similarly, the working together of our right and left hands illustrates how right and left, masculine and feminine, support and need each other.

I will look later at how, from the level of our physically one-sided bodies to our inner soul life, we can find a working together and inter-dependence of these two principles of feminine and masculine. Coming to know ourselves, we experience the polarity of feminine and masculine and also how that polarity makes a unity. It is clear that in all that we do these qualities must be able to work together. The feminine listens and questions, the masculine speaks and states. It moves and acts while the feminine waits, receptive and still. The masculine breaks apart, individualises and differentiates; the feminine brings together, generalises and finds similarities. These qualities are equally valuable and dependent upon each other for real creativity. To work towards self knowledge and to become receptive to our higher self leads through consciousness to wholeness. To create a physical child the union of male and female is necessary; to create an inner child, the child of the human spirit, we need a conscious union of feminine and masculine within. Today we begin to awaken to our inner androgyny, to the potential inner union of feminine and masculine.

The Ideal of Androgyny

The ideal of androgyny, the two in the one, lies at the foundation of our development. It marks the beginning and the end of time. In-between, what was once united separates into a duality to further evolution, but eventually the duality reunites to form a unity. Most creation myths, telling of a time beyond our knowing, giving us a glimpse of our origins and a premonition of our future, picture a state of divine oneness, a perfection resting in itself. In the beginning of all things, the great unconscious round (an empty circle and a full circle, a movement and a stillness) contains and joins all opposites. It is the womb of Paradise, the universal cosmic egg in which day and night, inner and outer, heaven and earth are one. Adam in the first chapter of Genesis is also created androgynous in the image of God; he is the archetypal, celestial human being, created in the image of the Elohim, male – female, both in one. Rudolf Steiner also speaks of a time of primeval wholeness at the beginning of earthly evolution, when all still rested in the "bosom of the godhead", in the "collective world womb". The forces of feminine and masculine in the earth were in union and human beings were unisexual, both male and female in one, and reproduced themselves through a kind of self-impregnating godly wisdom. [21]

The ideal of Androgyny reminds us of our original perfection and calls us to work towards it again in the freedom and consciousness we have gained through division. It is one of the oldest ideals of humanity, one that has existed in most cultures and societies, even in our Western Judeo-Christian culture, although here it has remained hidden and secret. Today, however, partly as a result of the general quest for renewed connection with the spirit, and partly through the research coming out of the Women's Movement, this universal ideal has begun to surface more. This points to the fact that behind all the struggles between and amongst women and men, lives a longing for and a movement towards union.

In the New Testament there are many images of our potential wholeness. Christ is a model of one who brings feminine and masculine wisdom into balance, one in whom love and wisdom flow together. In the *Galatians*, Paul says that in Christ "there is neither male nor female: for ye are all one in Christ Jesus". [22] In *Revelations* Christ says: "I am the alpha and the omega, the beginning and the ending". [23] He is the wholeness and perfection at the beginning and the end of earth evolution. He is the second Adam, the original and androgynous human being. He brings to earth a promise of a new unity, based on a free and selfless love that can flow between developed individuals, a new psychic love, free from physical and sense-based ties. Christ conquers death, which came into the world with the Fall and the division of opposites. His resurrection is a seed, a promise for a new and conscious union with the spirit, for the revelation and resurrection of the true human form which is independent of what William Blake calls our "sexual garments":

"These are the sexual garments, the Abomination of Desolation
Hiding the Human Lineaments as with an Ark and Curtains
Which Jesus rent and now shall wholly purge way with fire
Till Generation is swallow'd up in Regeneration."[24]

Rudolf Steiner says that Christ represents to humanity one who has established within himself harmony and concord between the maternal and the paternal principles. "Through Christ man was to find the possibility of establishing harmony within himself, of harmonising the antagonistic forces in his own inner being".[25] He says that this inner harmony between the maternal and the paternal principles was the great ideal in ancient times. The maternal principle generalises and creates resemblance between us and our fellow human beings. It is all we share in common with humanity, a principle of oneness and union through which we experience ourselves as part of a network of connections and relationships. The paternal principle individualises and makes us different and separate from each other; through it we stand alone. Steiner speaks of how, in the far past, an inner harmony between these two principles was not possible. Individuals who sought higher wisdom and the unity of all had to abandon their individual egos. But since Christ's coming, human beings have the possibility of finding a love and union without giving up their individuality, for Christ unites the masculine principle of individuality with the feminine principle of oneness. Thus He makes it possible for all who search to discover within themselves the balancing force of the true self.

The ideal of androgyny, of the wholeness of feminine and masculine, frequently and beautifully finds expression in the writings of the early Christian Gnostics. In their texts (secret gospels, revelations and mystical writings that were condemned as heretical and were excluded from the New Testament), God often appears as Androgynous, both father and mother in one, the Divine seen as a dynamic relationship of opposites. The feminine principle of the universe works creatively with the masculine, as women and men in early Christian worship worked together equally (women, like men, could lead worship and acted as prophets, teachers and evangelists). In the trinity of Father, Son and Holy Spirit, the Holy Spirit was often seen as feminine, the divine Sophia, the Mother of the world. In the *Apochryphon of John* this divine mother is described. "She is . . . the image of the invisible, virginal, perfect spirit . . . She became the Mother of everything, for she existed before them all, the mother – father".[26] In his studies on the *Luke Gospel*, Emil Bock speaks of how the Holy Spirit called up the picture of the Maria Sophia before the souls of early Christians. They knew that Mary, like Jesus, was not just a human being; as they found the Christ in Jesus, so in Mary they found the Holy Spirit. The wholeness of Christ and His Kingdom is also an ever-present theme in the Christian Gnostic texts, as in the following passage from the *Gospel according to Thomas*.

"Jesus saw children who were being suckled. He said to his disciples 'These children who are being suckled are like those who enter the Kingdom'. They said to him: 'Shall we then, being children, enter the Kingdom?' Jesus said to them: 'When you make the two one, and when you make the inner as the outer and the outer as the inner, and the above as the below, and when you make the male and the female into a single one, so that the male will not be male, and the female (not) be female . . . then shall you enter (the Kingdom).'"[27]

In the Middle Ages this ideal of balance surfaced again strongly in Christianity, particularly through the cult of the Madonna. In honouring Mary, Mother of the World and the wisdom of the world, the Holy Spirit was also honoured. Working behind the establishment of the cult of the Virgin, was the aim to find a new wholeness and to become finally independent of the sexes. Connected with the veneration of Mary at this time was the living vision of the Mother of the Earth, the goddess Natura, 'Vice-Regent of God', and the procreator of "the sublunary world". The awareness of the feminine, life-giving force that flows through all things was still strong, particularly in the school of Chartres. But even here, as a sign of the imbalance to come, Natura is pictured with her garment torn, weeping for the falling away of human beings from her care, and for the rape that scientific materialistic consciousness would bring.

The ideal of Androgyny also lived during this time in the work of the alchemists, in which the marriage of feminine and masculine was central. The essential elements in the alchemical process were often pictured in terms of the masculine and feminine polarity – sun and moon, king and queen, heaven and earth, male and female. Alchemical work needed both men and women; the adept and the soror/sister worked together, the man on the right and the woman on the left and the vessel between them. The process was called "the alchemical wedding". The alchemists knew that in order to transform themselves they had to call on both their feminine and masculine sides. The work required the whole human being.

The holistic approach characterised the way of working and the goals of the work; the way was also the goal. Alchemy was both a chemical and a spiritual process. In their investigation of nature, alchemists were at once scientific and objective, mystical and artistic. Their science was also an art. They prepared for their experiments in a laboratory by developing an inner purity and a strengthened morality. They worked with matter in order to discover the living substance behind it, so that interwoven with their science was the goal of developing vision. The alchemists wanted to find the spiritual in outer nature and in their own inner nature, and they knew that revelation in one area depended on activity in another. Their goal was, through the process of dissolution and union, to find the spiritual in the material (gold) and to become receptive to their own true sun-like nature. From a fusion of masculine and feminine energies, a new substance would be created. Called the Philosopher's Stone, the stone of love, the elixir of life, the diamond body, or the filius philosophorum, this new substance seems to have been the formation of Christ within. The alchemical vessel in which the transformation took place was the receptive human being and what was created was a higher, spiritual, androgynous self.

The image of feminine and masculine creating a single body also informs the ideal of marriage. In the Christian Community marriage service the ideal of wholeness is clearly expressed in the service. The Head of Christ by Leonardo da Vinci, a clear picture of a being who is neither masculine or feminine but both and more, is used to remind the woman and the man who are uniting their lives that marriage can be a path through which they can begin to overcome the division of the sexes. In the Anglican Book of Common Prayer, the woman and the man in marriage are said to become "one flesh" in the image of Christ in his Bride. Through their life and love there is a subtle mingling that forms one body, a higher, sexless androgynous body. John Donne in his poem *The Canonisation* writes that "To one neutral thing both sexes fit."[28] Perhaps it is a reflection of this mingling that women and men who have lived together for many years begin to look alike. It is this living, invisible bond that is also torn and hurt if there is a separation of two people through death or divorce. The tear and division of this substance that was once whole and once united two people, gives rise to feelings of disorientation and an almost physical pain, as if from an open wound. If we could become more aware of this, we would allow ourselves more healing time after a relationship ends before trying to form another one.

Another place where the ideal of androgyny was kept alive in the past was in the ancient Mystery Schools, where pupils underwent rigorous inner and outer exercises on a path that would lead them to an understanding of the meaning and mystery of existence. Rudolf Steiner describes the rituals of many of these schools and it has been interesting to me to find that an understanding of the mystery of the polarity of male and female in the cosmos and in the human being was often central to the path of initiation. This was particularly true in the Hibernian Mysteries as Steiner describes them.[29] Here after suitable preparation, the pupils were brought before two great statues, one representing the male, the other the female. This experience made a deep and powerful impression on the pupils and gave rise to many questions about the nature of this fundamental polarity of existence. The male statue was huge, and majestic because of its size; its head appeared as though formed out of the sun's rays. It was made of elastic material and was hollow inside; when pressed its form was always re-established. He spoke the following words:

> "I am the image of the world
> Behold how I lack being
> I live in thy knowledge
> I become now in thee consecration."

The female statue was smaller and seemed composed of luminous bodies radiating inwards and her head was produced out of these rays. She was less distinct than the male, and was made of soft and plastic material, so that if the statue was pressed the indentation remained and the form was destroyed. However, when the pupils returned later, the form was always restored. She spoke the following words to the pupils:

"I am the image of the world
Behold how I lack truth.
If thou wilt dare to live with me
I will be thy comfort."

Through these statues, pupils were led into the experience of the male and female polarity and of the extremes of one side and then the other. They came to feel what knowledge was without being, what fantasy was without truth, science without art. They experienced the extremes of living totally within sense experience, the past, and a harsh and cold and frozen winter landscape. Then they experienced equally intensely the opposite – the heat of a summer landscape, the inner warmth, the life of dream and fantasy, living always in the future.

Of course, for the pupils of the Mystery Schools, the actual path of initiation was much more complicated and profound than I am able to describe here. But, after a long time of living fully with the extremes of polarity, the pupils developed the need and the possibility of finding the middle, an inner force of balance, an androgynous oneness in their souls. The ultimate experience for the pupils was a meeting with the Christ who was yet to come, the One who could unite science and art, masculine and feminine, the past and the future, dream experience with sense experience; the One who would bring the possibility for all humanity of finding a force of peace within.

In some ways, the whole of our existence on earth is a continual movement, flow, tension, between opposites. It is the most fundamental experience of our lives, for the sense of ourselves only arises out of an interplay and interchange between polarity – day and night, outer and inner, dark and light, sleeping and waking, inhaling and exhaling, life and death, summer and winter, hot and cold. In between, we wake up and become conscious of the world and ourselves. We awaken to the sense of I, which then can be the harmoniser, that which holds the balance. Through our incarnation into polarity, we gain the capacity of ego-consciousness, with which we can find a way towards a new wholeness.

Today we do not need to go to a Mystery School to work with the feminine and masculine polarity, for life initiates us in the many-coloured workings of this polarity. There are many people who consciously seek to bring to expression and creative interaction both feminine and masculine qualities within themselves. Stimulated by the discussion coming out of the Women's Movement, people have begun to define themselves more fully, to include what has been excluded, the unconventional, the taboo, the feminine in a man, the masculine in a woman. They have experimented with roles in an effort to break down narrow role definitions and stereotyped expectations of the other. Basically, people long to fully express their humanity and be open to it in each other. They want to meet as individuals, and to find the realm of spiritual equality from which they can truly work for balance and in consciousness unite what has been so divided in individuals and society.

Rudolf Steiner pointed to the vital necessity of this inner work. He said that if, instead of focussing on the outer polarity, we begin to work on our inner balance, we will be able to divert the strife in the outer world and that from our inner work love and harmony will flow into the world. This was the ideal in ancient times. "To bring into harmonious relationship the father and mother in him was the great ideal. If this were not achieved , disharmony between the paternal and maternal elements would be reproduced outside on the physical plane, with disastrous effects. The old sage therefore taught: 'It is the duty of man to establish harmony within himself between the paternal and maternal elements. The failure to do so cannot but show itself in the outer world as the most appalling crimes.'"[30] So if we are able to recognise the imbalance around us as a reflection of our own inner disharmony, we can begin to work effectively towards a greater harmony within and without. Even though this seems to make us vulnerable, it also frees us and enables us to approach our full potential as women or men.

Women and Men _ similarities and differences

This union or inner androgyny that we seek, however, is not a blurring of feminine or masculine or the real differences between women and men. It is important that we do not try to deny the basic polarity of the sexes, or anticipate too soon their future reunification. Certainly it is not in the physical realm that we should look for union today, although it does filter through to this level (i.e. the unisex fashion in clothing), and some people would minimise or even deny our physical differences. But I think that most people today have an intuition of what was known in the old Mystery Schools – that for true harmony it is essential to also know the meaning and value of the differences between women and men – that in order to know balance, we have to also fully experience the opposites. We seek, then, to connect an appreciation of our incarnation into polarity with our growing sense that our true being is beyond this differentiation. It is this two-fold search that I want to consider now, first of all by exploring how we can begin to understand the differences between women and men and how the feminine and masculine polarity is at work in all of us and at all levels, from our physical bodies to our inner soul life.

Physically, the differences between women and men are obvious. Women embody the feminine pole and men embody the masculine pole; they complement each other and need each other to reproduce. In a woman the feminine principle works in her physical body, which is generally soft, round, flexible, receptive, vulnerable and open. It has the capacity for transformation; when a woman is pregnant her whole body becomes a vessel, a temple, protecting, nourishing, containing the developing child within, receptive to the secrets of the cosmos and the creative powers of the universe. In the male, the masculine works outwardly; his body is physically more condensed, firm and muscular; it is penetrating, linear, differentiated. The female form is more generalised and inward, while the male form is more individualised and outward.

In a series of lectures entitled *Embryology and World Evolution* Dr. Karl König, the founder of the Camphill Movement, speaks of how the fruit-bearing organs of women and men contain and reflect these two poles of existence. "The ovary is a relatively stable organ. The testes, the testicle, is a tremendously vital organ. Everything the testes produces is always new. Millions and millions of sperm cells are, one might say, continuously begotten and created within it. It is a fountain head of continual and unending vitality. On the other hand, when a girl is born the ovary already contains the total number of germs, only some of which will gradually develop in the course of her life. The ovaries lie within the body, they are, so to speak, more or less held in position at the end of the abdominal cavity, though remaining in a state of suspension. That is the gesture of the female pole. The testes on the other hand emerges from the body, it breaks out of the outer form of the abdomen and descends, must move downwards, when the man reaches maturity. With that . . . the testes falls under the influence of gravity. Fundamentally it becomes a limb, not a perfect one, but nevertheless a limb . . . There is a quality of suspension, maintenance, bearing power, preservation in the female organism; and something of a fountain head which is yet under the influence of gravity and has wrested itself free from the body in the male generative organ."[31]

In the same lecture cycle, Dr. König also speaks of the correspondence between the egg developing in an ovary (the Graafian follicle) and the structure of the primitive ears and balancing organs of the lower animals. The egg is a kind of ear, travelling through darkness, listening and waiting for the right moment of conception. Thus the feminine qualities of listening, balancing, receiving, work within the forms and processes of women's physical bodies. Dr. König draws attention to the remarkable similarity between the Eustachian tube (the passage from the throat to the ears) and the Fallopian tube (the passage that leads from the cavity of the uterus to the point near the ovary). These two passages were even discovered within a year of each other (by Eustacchi in 1524 and Fallopio in 1523). There is a definite correspondence between female and ear, and between hearing and conception. Thinking about the connection between the feminine quality of listening and the femaleness of the ear, I thought of how women, even when they are sound asleep, will hear the slightest sound their babies make in another room. Although this is more than a physical hearing, studies have confirmed the connection between women and good hearing. "Females also hear better than males: their auditory discrimination and localisation is superior at all ages. Males, on the other hand, see better. These sex-typical advantages in sensory capacities are not learned or acquired through particular forms of experience; they are evident in infancy. Even at a few weeks of age, boys show more interest in visual patterns, while the infant girls attend more to tonal sequences."[32]

Dr. König also stresses the correspondence between the male and the eye. ". . . from the point of view of comparative anatomy, and also pathological anatomy, it is so, that the ear and the ovary, the eye and the testes bear a deep relationship to each other. There are certain eye diseases which affect men only, e.g. colour blindness, but quite a few other things as well, for this very reason that the eye is specifically male, and the ear very much a female organ."[33]

Rudolf Steiner speaks of how, at the division of the sexes, the human beings who became female took a body for themselves that bore the stamp of imagination, whereas the male form was conditioned more by the element of will. (It is important to remember that the time he is speaking of, the Lemurian Epoch, is at the very beginning of earthly evolution, when physical records and even physical bodies as we know them did not exist.) This physical division into male and female was then cultivated and enhanced by the different trainings for boys and girls. Boys were educated to develop their will faculty. They were hardened by exposure to the elements, and they were made to undergo great dangers, to perform daring and courageous deeds, and to overcome pain and discomfort. Girls on the other hand were trained to develop strong, imaginative capacities, they were encouraged in their propensity to evolve a rich dream and fantasy life.

Women have the capacity to conceive and bear a child, to nurture, sustain, maintain life. Through the menstrual cycle, a woman has a direct connection to rhythm, so that she cannot easily forget the real relation of the human being to the rhythms of nature and the cosmos. The menstrual cycle is an internalised lunar rhythm, no longer directly dependent on the changes of the moon but still bearing a relationship to those phases (the average length of the menstrual cycle is 29.5 days which is the same as the period from new moon to new moon). This basic life sustaining rhythm has been disturbed in our time. However, in recent years many women have begun to realise the dangers of interfering with this cycle particularly through the birth control pill. A growing number of women have expressed their desire to find a better connection to and a new respect for their bodies. Arising out of this there have been different studies looking at the deeper meaning of menstruation. These studies suggest that women are very lucky to have such a cycle, for it keeps us in touch with our bodies, the earth and the stars. Rather than being a nuisance or a curse, menstruation is an unexplored female resource, essential to our minds as well as to our bodies, important in establishing a relationship to our deepest self. Through our cycle we remember the interconnections of all things, even our feminine and masculine qualities. In the course of a month, many women recognise a time of a more diffuse consciousness, of heightened receptivity, openness and waiting, and another time of tension, self-assertiveness, clarity and quickness. Thus, to be in tune with our cycle opens us toward our potential wholeness.

Karl König's lectures on *Embryology and World Evolution* are an important contribution to this attempt to understand the significance of the menstrual cycle. He considers this cycle in connection with the Biblical story of creation and with Rudolf Steiner's ideas about cosmic and earthly evolution. He suggests that the movement and preparation of the egg for fertilisation is a recapitulation of the coming into being of the earth and humanity, that stored within our monthly cycle is a kind of cosmic memory, a record of past earth history. To tamper with this rhythm, then, may be to cut off a recollection in the physical of the working of the spirit, just at this time when we are in great need of re-finding a strong and clear relationship to the spirit.

The male carries the individualising force. If women could reproduce themselves their offspring would all be female and all look alike. In early embryological development if a child is to be female it follows a fairly direct path, unfolding a natural tendency to be female. If the child is to be male, however, differentiation must occur to overcome and separate from this innate femaleness of the embryo and the whole maternal environment. It must differentiate and fight to become male.

"Only the male embryo is required to undergo the differentiating transformation of the sexual anatomy: . . . Female development pursues a straight course with the reproductive organs not subject to any hormonal differentiating transformation. Foetal and maternal estrogens merely enhance, and this later, slowly and to a relatively moderate degree, the already unfolding female morphology. On the other hand, strong activity from foetal androgen is necessary to change the female morphology into the masculine pattern."[34]

There is yet another way to look at this basic difference in the physical nature of women and men. Rudolf Steiner speaks of how, at the time of the division of the sexes, female nature chose a body for itself which did not come far enough into materiality but retained an earlier, more spiritual form. Of course it became material, but it was more flexible; it was less earth-bound, less dense or intense than the male nature, which penetrated too far, too deeply into matter. Therefore, Steiner says: "The true human form would fall between the two and would consist of a happy average of both."[35]

According to Steiner, this difference influences our whole thinking life and the way we meet and work with the events and experiences of our lives. Because the form of the male brain is so deeply materialised, it is more rigid and difficult to manage than the more flexible form of the female brain. It is an instrument of intellect and more connected to the will than the imaginative, feeling life. It is more adapted to materialistic thinking; it is good at dealing with the surfaces of things, with the physical plane, but it has difficulty following more subtle channels of thought. It is "frozen to a certain degree",[36] and does not easily free itself from fixed patterns of thought. In general then, men have the capacity to be precise and exact and centred in their thinking. They can concentrate and can formulate things, but their thinking can also become dry and abstract, cut off from the life around. Steiner says: "Any man knows that the male brain is frequently an intractable instrument. On account of its rigidity it offers terrible resistance when one would use it for more flexible lines of thought. It refuses to follow and must be educated by all sorts of means before it can lose its rigidity. With all men this can be a personal experience."[37] And, in another place: "If people had even the smallest inkling of what it means to think in the spirit, to live in the spirit, using the physical body only as an instrument so that one does not feel firmly fastened into and identified with it, they would sing songs about the misery of having to use a male body in an incarnation because these material effects have of course also filtered into the brain . . . It is truly more difficult to train a male brain for the ascent into higher worlds, and to translate truths into thoughts, than it is to train a female brain."[38]

The female brain is more flexible and pliable; its thinking is warmer, softer, more spiritually open and free, closer to inspirational wisdom. Because of this, women are often receptive to newly appearing or revolutionary ideas; they grasp spiritual ideas quickly and are often first to accept new spiritual impulses (i.e. early Christianity, Jungian psychology, Anthroposophy). They have a capacity to accept and understand the unusual. Steiner suggests that this is one reason why Mary Magdalen is the first to see the Risen Christ.

A woman lives more strongly than a man in her emotional, soul life; experiences and events impress themselves deeply upon her inner being. Her thinking tends to be intuitive and subtle; she is aware of all the shades of meaning, all the things unexpressed as well as those expressed. She has a freer relationship to the external world and the world of ideas than a man. Her thinking can be creative and imaginative, but it also can be fantastic, with little connection to reality. A woman can easily invent her own truth.

It is important to remember that these differences apply only to female or male nature in general, not to individuals – otherwise we may find ourselves in the same situation as the Professor that Steiner tells us about who occupied himself with measuring human brains. He found that in general women's brains were smaller than those of men, and he concluded that, since a smaller brain must indicate less intelligence, women must be less intelligent than men. It seems he became famous for this discovery, but when he died and an autopsy was performed on him, it turned out that his brain was smaller than all the women's brains he had examined![39]

Flexibility does not belong exclusively to women, nor does materialistic thinking belong only to men. We all have the potential to develop a more willed, intellectual thinking and a more fluid, imaginative thinking. In fact, our creative development depends on finding a synthesis between these two modes of thinking. I would say that both women and men today have developed one-sidedly a rather dry, abstract thinking, an intellectual surface consciousness which does not move us beyond a literal, mechanical understanding of things. Our thinking has become frozen and intractable; it refuses to follow. The feminine knows how to follow; it knows how to follow the spirit and so it can lead us back to the spirit. It can enliven our feeling life and bring a flexibility, warmth and subtlety to our thinking life. If we can find a synthesis between feminine and masculine, a creative balance between intellect and imagination, we begin to work towards what Rudolf Steiner calls the transformation of head wisdom through the heart, the bringing together of the head with the heart so that we build a bridge between our thinking and our doing.

I will return to this theme of balance, but I want to look further still at the differences (and similarities) between women and men. However, perhaps it is important to point out here that, though there is no denying the gap between the physical form of women and men, even in the physical body there is a continual integration and harmony between feminine and masculine. Earlier I mentioned the working together of the right and left hands, and the right and left sides of the brain, as a possible image of the feminine and masculine in balance. This can also be observed in a person's face; often the left side is softer, less defined, more inward-looking, more feminine, and the right side is clearer, sharper, more wilful-looking, more masculine. In a different way, Dr. König illustrates how the head unites the feminine and masculine forces which fall apart "in analysis in the body below".

In his drawing of the human face (see illustration above), he shows how there is a synthesis of the moon-like, feminine principle, contained in the ears and mouth, and the masculine, sun-like, vitalising principle contained in the eyes and the nose. These two principles held in harmony in every human face are then "torn apart, and down below become, so to speak, the male and the female power."[40]

In the human body the glands fall into pairs which control complementary qualities and mutually balance each other. For example, the pituitary gland has two lobes, the posterior and the anterior pituitary. The posterior lobe controls the involuntary muscles of the inner instinctive part of the body, especially those of the intestines, the bladder and the uterus. It also regulates the production of milk and is generally the gland of maternal qualities. The anterior pituitary, on the other hand, promotes more masculine traits. It is closely connected with both the skeletal system and the function of abstract thought and reason.

Both women and men produce both female and male hormones, though with a preponderance of one or the other. The genetic code for humans calls for a certain proportion of each hormone, with the result that males and females are not very different. In other species the imbalance is so great that male and female seem hardly to belong to the same species. The hormone ratio is also not fixed but shifts throughout our lives. For example, at puberty girls begin to produce more female hormones and boys more male hormones, but as women and men approach old age this level changes again and there is less difference between women and men. In between these two points, alternations in hormone levels probably depend on many things, both physiological and psychological. For example, a woman's inner state is obviously affected by the course of her menstrual cycle and the changing hormone levels connected with it. It is well known that her feelings can affect her cycle; if she is excited or nervous in anticipation of some coming event, menstruation may occur earlier than expected. Fear or violence, or an overly intellectual life-style can inhibit menstruation. Studies have also been made that show that women who work closely together or live together menstruate at the same time, somehow tuning in to each other's rhythms.

The masculine and feminine balance is, of course, not just a matter of hormone level. In his book *Phases* Bernard Lievegoed speaks of this male and female balance in all individuals. "Biologically, man is constructed on a bisexual framework. The primitive kidney which lays down the entire urogenital system during the early embryonic period develops, for a time, both organ systems, until there comes a moment when maleness or femaleness gains the upper hand, and the organs of the opposite sex cease development. In the adult man and woman it is possible to see the remains of the embryonic organisation of the opposite sex. For instance, the mammary glands are initially present in both man and woman, but only develop fully in the female."[41]

Biologically we are all bisexual and the potential that does not come to physical expression continues to influence us from the unconscious. Awareness of this duality and the development of one side of ourselves and the holding back of the other, leads to differences in how we experience our being. We all exist somewhere on a continuum between pure femaleness and pure maleness, between the 'he-man', masculine, 'macho'-male, and the dainty, flower-like, feminine woman. There are various possible gradations in between, and we all have our own particular mix, which can change and shift throughout our life. Highly one-sided people, either extremely male or extremely female, can be limited in their inner experience and may view the world through a narrow lens. They may have difficulty in understanding the differences of the other sex, for we understand the other through the recognition and understanding of the other within ourselves. If individuals cannot accept and include this other within themselves, half of the world remains unknowable to them. This can also make it harder for them to have a true sense of themselves as independent of their sex, and they may be met by others chiefly as a woman or man. Thus it may be harder for very one-sided people to come to inner balance, whereas people with a more even balance and sense of themselves as male-female (which still does not confuse sexual identity) have the possibility of a fuller, richer inner life and a deeper understanding of others.

Rudolf Steiner adds another dimension to this picture of balance. He says that as well as a physical body, human beings have an etheric body, a life body, which sustains and maintains the physical body. The etheric body is the architect of the physical, imbuing it with life and form. It is a body of living, constantly-moving, inter-flowing forces. "The etheric body appears like a form of light extending everywhere but only slightly beyond the form of the physical body. The human being has the etheric body in common with the plants."[42]

Steiner says that in our etheric body we find a kind of residue of our ancient dual sex, for a man's etheric body is female, and a woman's etheric body is male; we carry the image of the other within. The opposite sex dwells hidden within each person. "If you could think away the physical body, you would see that the etheric body, especially in the upper parts, is almost similar to the physical body. This similarity, however, continues only as far as the middle of the body for there is great differentiation within the etheric body; you will realise that this is so when I tell you that the etheric body in the male is female, and in the female, male. Without this knowledge much will remain incomprehensible in practical life."[43]

This picture of balance makes it clear why it is important not just to speak of woman and man, but of feminine and masculine qualities that work either within or without. In women the feminine pole works outwardly, while the masculine works more inwardly. In a man, the opposite is the case – the masculine works outward into the world, into the physical, while his feminine nature is more inward. Another way Steiner describes this is by looking at the influence of the sun and the moon on women and men. He says that a woman's physical body is more strongly influenced by the moon while the sun forces are more active in her etheric body. The opposite is true for a man – the moon forces work strongly in his etheric body while the sun forces have a more direct influence on his physical body.

The picture of human nature as the working together of two polar opposites helps us to understand why it is not only difficult but often misleading when we try to fix the characteristics of women and men, or even of the feminine and masculine polarity. When we try to define a woman as this or that, are we seeing the feminine in her or her masculine counterpart? Is the inward working of the masculine in a woman different from its outer manifestation in a man? How does the feminine express itself in a man? How is that different from the feminine in a woman? These are the questions that are not easy to answer but are important to hold in mind, otherwise we slip into over-simplification. Rudolf Steiner emphasized this point in the lectures he gave on this theme, as in the following passages:

"A very noteworthy scientist of the 19th century described the basic quality of woman to be humility. Another, whose comment is equally valid, declared it to be an angry disposition. Another scientist, who sparked off much controversy, came to the conclusion that the female nature is basically submissive, while yet another felt that it consisted of the desire to dominate. One described women as conservative, and still another felt women to be the true revolutionary element in the world. . .

"This quaint collection could be extended indefinitely, though in the end one would only learn that through looking at things on a purely external level, intelligent people are led to opposite conclusions. . . One cannot merely look at externalities, rather one must consider the whole being of the human being . . .

". . . So long as one merely looks at the physical body little can be understood. The spiritual lying behind must also be recognised. Through his masculine nature the inner femininity of the man appears, and through the woman's feminine nature her inner masculinity appears. Now one can grasp why it is that so many misjudgments have been made about this question; it depends on whether one looks at the inner, or the outer, aspects. Considering only one side of the human being, one is subjected entirely to chance. Error must occur with this kind of approach. In order to recognise the full truth we must look at the whole human being."[44]

In trying to understand the differences of sex of our physical and etheric bodies, it is helpful to keep in mind that the etheric body itself is whole. It is both feminine and masculine, but one half works strongly into the physical body and forms and builds up that body; the other half, the feminine in a man and the masculine in a woman, is freer and works more to build up the inner soul life and the life of thought. On a physical level, women are receptive and open, and more vulnerable than men. Their strength lies inwardly, in sacrifice, nurturing, and devotion; their life of ideas and imagination is strong in an inner sense. Men, through their physical bodies have an outer strength and courage; their ideas and creativity are engaged with the external world. Through their female etheric, they are inwardly sensitive and vulnerable.[45]

In looking at how the feminine and masculine polarity works in us, it is important to remember that our physical and etheric bodies constitute our outer sheaths. They make us a man or a woman. But this outer determination has nothing to do with our spiritual being or essence. It is this essence, or individuality, that we long to meet and express more and more today and which increasingly determines our path through life. Yet, on the other hand, the outer garment we wear does affect how our spirit manifests, the experiences which come to us in life, and how we meet those experiences. Our biology does affect our soul life.

Many people today struggle with the tension between their growing consciousness of their individuality and their need to understand and live fully into the particular sex that they are. I know myself as a woman, in my various roles as daughter, sister, wife, mother, but I also have another sense of myself as independent of these roles and of my sex, of this body I wear almost like clothing, this "sexual garment". Many people want to know: Why am I a woman? Why am I a man? What am I doing in this body now? What does it mean for my development? What are my tasks as a woman, or a man? These questions point to our need to find a way to bring together a sense of individuality with an acceptance and understanding of the differences between women and men.

I have found that Rudolf Steiner's picture of the individual human ego and his ideas about karma and reincarnation offer a way to understand and bridge our sense of individuality with our sense of ourselves as modern women and men. Our ego, our spiritual individuality, is above the level of the sexes and expresses the true human being; it is the same in both women and men. It is this essential being in all of us which reincarnates throughout earthly evolution and chooses sometimes to be a woman and sometimes to be a man because the different experiences of each sex are so important to the growth and full expression of the developing individual and for a full experience of earthly conditions.

"The period required by the sun for its passage through one zodiacal constellation is the period within which the human being is twice incarnated, once as a man and once as a woman. The experiences in a male and female organism are so fundamentally different for spiritual life that the human being incarnates once as a woman and once as a man into the same conditions of the earth . . ."

"As a rule, the sex alternates. This rule, however, is often broken, so that sometimes there are three to five, but never more than seven, consecutive incarnations in the same sex."[46]

This is a wonderful picture of our intention for balance, of the human being as a spirit being evolving through time, bringing feminine and masculine wisdom into harmony. I think many people can respond to such an image and recognise it to be true to what they most deeply know – that our true humanity lies between male and female. Such a picture can free us and help us not to limit ourselves and others by sexual stereotypes. It allows us to live into the differences between women and men without feeling trapped or judged by those differences, for if we are women now we know we have been men before and will be again, and vice versa. It is all part of our search for balance over time, our gradual learning to express our full humanity. It can also foster a sense of responsibility, a sense that perhaps the conditions I am meeting now in my life as a man or a woman I have set up. We may wonder, for example, if the women who today are struggling to harmonize and warm our overly masculine culture were men at the time when this masculine culture was being established and that they now must bring the balance to that which they created.

The law of karma works in such a way that we are always moving towards balance, wanting to compensate for our one-sidedness and to see and know the world as fully as possible. If we are women this means that we strive to become men in our next incarnation, and if we are men we long to become women.

"What we prepare in one incarnation will be an organising force for our body in the next . . . Thus we must say the fact of having a man's or a woman's experience in one incarnation, in one way or another, determines our external deeds in the next incarnation."[47]

Rudolf Steiner says that a woman's soul is profoundly influenced by experiences and events, whereas they do not enter so deeply in a man's life. A woman is touched deeply by all that goes on around her, and this tendency in her creates a longing to be more fully incarnated into matter. Thus in her next life this longing works to form a male body. A man, on the other hand, generally does not penetrate too far below the surface of things. This tendency works then to form a female body in the next life – a body less deeply incarnated. Thus through our experiences in one life as a woman or a man we build our body for the next life. "Man is woman's karma" and "Woman is man's karma".[48]

In some ways then, the polarity between female and male (and feminine and masculine) that exists in linear time becomes somewhat illusory when we consider our lives in terms of development through time, for the one constantly moves towards and flows into the other, the one contains the other. Perhaps too, as we work to harmonise ourselves throughout cycles of time, we eventually come to a point in evolution when the inner nature of women and men becomes more whole, less one-sided. However, as long as we are women and men, this picture of reincarnation and karma suggests that we choose a female or male body for particular experiences and opportunities. Thus the question arises: what does it mean for an individual that they are a woman, or a man? What do I want to experience, meet, learn and develop that I would be unable to do if I were a man? What are my possibilities, my limitations and my responsibilities? I would like now to explore some general responses to these questions.

The Meaning of Being a Man or a Woman

Today a growing number of men ask: "Why am I a man?" Many experience a crisis in their identity as men and in their relationship to the masculine. This crisis has different causes. The Women's Movement and the growing confidence and strength of women has made some men feel threatened and insecure about what they have to offer to the world and their relationships. Their deeper materiality has become more of a burden today, as people begin to search for ways to free themselves from materialism and to find a new relationship to the spiritual dimension of reality.

In any case, women have made a stronger connection to the earth today; they go out to work and can achieve and provide, and cope with the physical world. So work itself, through which men have always defined their masculinity, no longer provides them with a sure identity. This is especially true as there is less value on, and less opportunity and need for, physical labour. And rising unemployment means that many men are unable to find any work at all. There are positive aspects of this situation which I will consider later, but I think it is true to say that all of this can make men feel very fearful and vulnerable, especially if they are always blamed for all the problems in the world. Men can feel very confused – the 'New Age' and the feminine are seen as exciting and positive, while everything about the masculine can appear 'bad' or problematic. So they want to give it up, to deny their masculinity and develop the feminine within. The urge to develop the feminine side of themselves is of course an important and positive development in men, part of their search for wholeness. But there is also a problem if men begin to turn away from the masculine and withdraw from the world, reluctant to face the things of the world, to make decisions, to take initiative. For what does it mean to have a male incarnation?

Rudolf Steiner says that men have a stronger relationship to the physical and the ego, that a male incarnation is 'physical divine'. We can understand this if we think of how boys develop – how they awaken through their intellect and will, their thinking and their doing, while their feeling life is more unknown. Boys and men often love wrestling and sports. They are at home in the material world and enjoy working their will into matter; they love to tinker with things and machines. Often men friends like to walk together, play ball together, and talk about ideas together. Steiner also speaks of how children choose their father as a guide to earthly conditions, as an example of how the ego or individuality can develop on the earth.

Although these indications apply to men in general, not to individuals, they seem to point to the fact that a male incarnation is about developing a strong and clear relationship to the masculine, about experiencing the power of the spirit working into and through the physical, without violence or anarchy. Being a man is a challenge to develop a clear awareness of self and the world, to work with the things of the world and, with clarity of thought, to penetrate and transform the physical world.

Robert Bly, in an interview in the journal *New Age* called "What Men Really Want", speaks about the necessity for men today to find a relationship to their masculine qualities. When asked "What's going on with men these days?", he answers:

"No-one knows! Historically the male has changed considerably in the past 30 years. Back then there was a person we could call the 50s male, who was hard-working, responsible, fairly well disciplined; he didn't see women's souls very well though he looked at their bodies a lot. Reagan still has this personality. The 50s male was vulnerable to collective opinion: if you were a man you were supposed to like football games, be aggressive, stick up for the U.S., never cry, and always provide. But this image of the male lacked feminine space. It lacked some sense of flow; it lacked compassion.

"Then during the 60s another sort of male appeared. The waste and anguish of the Vietnam War made men question what an adult male really is. And the Women's Movement encouraged men to actually look at women, forcing them to become conscious of certain things that the 50s male tended to avoid. As men began to look at women and at their concerns some men began to see their own feminine side and pay attention to it. That process continues to this day, and I would say that most young males are now involved in it to some extent.

"Now there's something wonderful about all this – the step of the male bringing forth his own feminine consciousness is an important one – and yet I have the sense that there is something wrong. . .

"I see the phenomenon of what I would call the 'Soft Male' all over the country today. Sometimes when I look out at my audience, perhaps half the young males are what I would call soft. They are lovely, valuable people – and they are not interested in harming the earth, starting wars, or working for corporations. There's something favourable towards life in their whole general mood and style of living.

"But something's wrong. Many of these men are unhappy. There's no energy in them. They are life-preserving but not exactly life-giving. And why is it that you often see these men with strong women, who positively radiate energy? Here we have a finely tuned young man, ecologically superior to his father, sympathetic to the whole harmony of the universe, and yet he himself has no energy to offer."[49]

Bly goes on to look at some reasons for the loss of masculine identity in men today – one of which he sees as the lack of a strong father image. Many boys today grow up without a father or, if they have a father, he is mostly absent, working at something the boy cannot understand and imitate. The father/son bond, so strong in pre-industrial times where the son worked alongside the father, has been broken, and with this the initiation into what it means to be a man has fallen away. So Bly suggests that men today have a task of finding a new relationship to the masculine – not the shallow 'macho'-masculine of brute force, but the deeply nourishing, spiritually-radiant energy of the masculine, a masculine which allows forceful, resolute and compassionate interaction.

On the surface, women today seem to be more at peace with being female. Through the Women's Movement we have found a voice in the world and support from each other; we have gained a certain strength and confidence. In the early 70s, many more women seemed to be asking themselves the questions: Why am I a woman? What am I meant to do in this body? Often they expressed their experience of surprise at finding themselves in a woman's body, wondering what it had to do with them. Today men seem to be asking about the meaning of being men with the same kind of urgency, while women appear to have gained more clarity of purpose.

However, there are still many questions and confusions. Many women are caught by a set of double expectations. We are taught and encouraged to be clear, focussed and independent. We are expected to work into the world to develop a career and compete as an equal (or even superior) to men. At the same time, we are expected to be (and expect ourselves to be) soft, warm, sensitive, nurturing, self-sacrificing, always available wives, lovers, mothers.

The problems relating to new forms of freedom have also become more apparent. In the early days of the Women's Movement, much attention was given to breaking down the old restrictions and expectations of the traditional female role. The voluntary care of children, the family, the institutions and traditions of society – a role in which women seemed to be sleeping and enslaved, was increasingly undervalued by society. But in attempting to wake women up to their individuality and in the ensuing struggle for equal rights in the political and economic realms, the Movement did much to continue the undermining and undervaluing of women's traditional roles (particularly motherhood) and the feminine qualities of caring, nurturing, serving, allowing. Some phases of the Movement seemed only to underline the dominant view that motherhood was a bind and a drudge, uncreative and unfulfilling, and that liberation meant liberation from the home and child-rearing. Freedom, self-development, creativity, and recognition were not achieved at home with the children, only in 'real' jobs in the 'real' outside world. Being a mother was unliberated and unfulfilling; it was something to apologise for.

Not only did the Movement seem to undervalue motherhood, but its voice was often harsh and strident, encouraging women to take on the hard, head-orientated, materialistic values that at a deeper level it longed to overcome, fostering the polarisation and isolation that it arose to heal. By extolling competition, aggression and material gain, by seeming to value only those skills leading to money, status, power, the Movement encouraged women to put on a masculine cloak and call it emancipation. This stance alienated many women who were struggling to find the meaning and significance in their work as mothers that they knew was there. In others, it called for a defensive reaction, a retreat from liberation and consciousness into a kind of sentimental and instinctive femininity. Thus, there are some women today who look to re-find security in the old stereotypes, roles and values, who want to rely on the old authority and morality of the past; they would make it a moral necessity for women to stay at home and give up the element of choice and freedom that they have won.

For many women, the particular emphasis of the Women's Movement, together with the masculine-orientated values and education of our time has created confusion about the meaning of being a woman. Differences between women and men have become blurred, or even denied. This is not to say that the masculine development in women or society is negative. As with the development of the feminine in men, the expression of the masculine in women has been a positive development, part of our struggle to become fuller, more balanced individuals. We certainly cannot or should not regret this masculine quality in women, or withdraw from it in society. But for many women, the masculine orientation of our times, together with women's struggle for equality and recognition, has meant a covering over, a denial of real sides of themselves. They have taken on masculine values as their own and denied their deeper and essential feminine qualities.

This problem was clearly expressed in an interview in *The Guardian* in 1978 called the "Chains of Liberation". The interview was with a woman who had been involved in the beginning and more militant side of the Women's Movement. After her second abortion, she became increasingly "despairing and depressed in her liberated existence". After trying to find "acceptable reasons" (in terms of her feminist principles) for her misery, she finally admits to herself that she has been living a lie.

"What I had been doing was grieving for the child I had lost, and painfully coming to realise that the woman I had created was actually a deliberate deformity of my real self.

"I realised with relief and horror mixed up together that I was a lot of things I had spent 10 years despising with all my heart. I actually yearned to spend whole days gurgling at a baby instead of arguing with intelligent and articulate contemporaries . . . I lusted after a built-in kitchen with gingham curtains and a huge diary on the wall filled with entries about point-to-points and P.T.A. meetings. God help us, I wanted a husband . . . The ludicrous thing about all this is that I am not saying anything sensible about what is wrong with the Women's Movement, or reverting back to silly notions about the True Nature of Women. What I am saying is that I missed the whole point of feminism right from the beginning. I got it wrong and muddled up and neurotic, and tied myself up in knots as a result. . .

"I continued to behave like a hysterical adolescent right up until after my 30th birthday, pouring a whole lot of debris from my own childhood jealousies and insecurities into the cause of liberation. With supporters like me, what movement needs opponents.

"I hope, I hope that I have now finished veering from extremes of fiction and misunderstanding. I believe women are still oppressed and exploited, and brought up to stifle their true creativity. I believe there are great sources of life and love to be found in other women, and there is still a lot of healthy, just anger to be voiced about the roles into which women are forced.

"But I also see now that I – and I don't think I am alone in this – used feminism as a protection against realities about myself that I could not face truthfully . . . But once you become aware of female consciousness there is no going back. My only hope is to start out along the road to liberation and self-confidence all over again when I feel less ashamed to face my own sex."[50]

It was partly the recognition of this growing confusion in women towards their own sex, the undervaluing of traditional female roles, the increased stresses and strains of illnesses suffered by women, seemingly from taking on more masculine roles, that led Betty Friedan to write *The Second Stage*. Interviewing young women in America, she found that many put off having children or becoming involved in a long term committed relationship, for fear of losing the independence and self-esteem which they had gained from their careers. They felt that to have a family would be a betrayal of their liberated principles, that they would become like their mothers – dissatisfied, undervalued housewives. These women then find themselves in their 30s with a successful career but with no real sustaining relationships, and feel another kind of enslavement. They begin to wonder whether they have missed out on life. This situation is apparent from the following quotations from interviews that Betty Friedan includes in her book.

"Even in that 'New Girls' network of women who have broken through the executive suite and enjoyed the tokens of professional and political equality I sense the exhilaration of 'superwomen' giving way to a tiredness and a certain brittle disappointment, the disillusionment with 'assertiveness training' and the rewards of power. Matina Horner, the high-powered president of Radcliffe, calls it a 'crisis of confidence'.

"An older woman in Ohio reflects: 'I was the first woman in management here. I gave everything to the job. It was exciting at first, breaking in where women never were before. Now it is just a job. But it is the devastating loneliness that is the worst. I cannot stand coming back to this apartment alone every night. I would like a house, maybe a garden. Maybe I should have a kid, even without a father. At least then I would have a family. There has to be some better way to live. A woman alone . . .'

"A woman who works in a bank in Chicago says: 'My husband takes more responsibility for the children now than I do. He also does all the cooking. I don't feel guilty. I just feel sorry that I do not see more of the children. A job is not the end. Larry used to make a lot more money than I do, but he hated what he was doing. I didn't see why it always had to be on him. It was exciting to get my job. The hard part is staying when you discover it is just a job, that you don't really like what you are doing.'"[51]

There seem to be many similar stories. Looking at the growing unhappiness in women and the imbalance, the undervaluing of the feminine in society, Betty Friedan calls for a second stage of the Women's Movement which would give more attention to family life, the choice to have children, and the work of caring for relationships. She encourages women to search for ways to avoid either-or choices – that we are either single and independent, or married and dependent, that we either have a child or a career, work or a family. She thinks that women can live out their own values without giving up the consciousness or the dignity they have won.

In contrast to men, Steiner says that women are more 'soul divine'; they have a stronger relationship to their inner nature, the etheric and astral bodies; they live strongly in the psychic, emotional realm. Steiner also speaks of how a child chooses its mother particularly for her soul qualities, for her inner imaginative life. A woman's strong connection to her soul life reveals itself in puberty, and is clearly apparent if we observe the differences between girls and boys at this time. While a boy's individuality remains more hidden, independent and apart from his developing emotional life, a girl's sense of self is strongly connected to her personal feelings and emotions. She really awakens in her feeling life and quite early has a certain capacity to express her thoughts and feelings, to announce herself to the world in a direct and forthright manner. She likes to spend hours talking about her feelings. This deep connection to the soul life (and the capacity to explore it) generally remains strong in women. They are at home in the realm of relationships, atmosphere and tone; they give priority to matters of the heart, and they have a deep connection to rhythm, nurturing, healing.

Many women today have strongly developed wills and intellects. They are self-conscious, clear-thinking, articulate, and have a capacity for precision, organisation, and criticism. They have developed and learned to express their masculine qualities. In asking why they are women, it may be that they need to uncover and bring to consciousness and expression the storehouse of feminine qualities within – to soften their judgment, bring a grace to their gestures, awaken to rhythm, and learn to give again out of the strong sense of self which they have developed.

The growth of the masculine in women can serve the renewal of their feminine qualities. Certainly the old instinctive feminine no longer answers our needs today. Women need to wake up and find purpose and direction. We need to develop our power of observation, to bring a greater objectivity and clarity to our inner imaginative, intuitive life, to bring more form and control to our feeling life. We need to join our love of fantasy with a love of truth. By calling on our newly developed masculine qualities to help us uncover and transform the feminine within us, we will be able to bring a truly awakened feminine into the many situations where this is needed today.

The growth of women's groups and friendships has encouraged this development. By sharing their experiences, women have begun to build new pictures of what our challenges and responsibilities are. Also, by trying to find new ways of working together, through all the listening, supporting and caring for each other, women have found a new trust and confidence in the feminine in themselves and in others, and they have begun to find ways of combining consciousness with caring, clarity with affection, honesty with warmth.

Discovering the meaning of being in a woman's body will of course be a personal search for every individual woman. But women today also have a sense of their collective task and responsibility that has come with the rights they have won. I touched on this question at the beginning of this chapter when I looked at the growing search among women to combine their now-awakened political consciousness with commitment to their true spiritual values and longings, and the broadening of women's issues to include the concerns of the whole of humanity. In this shift of emphasis, I believe women are beginning to awaken to their vital role in the future development of the earth. If we have a deep connection to those feminine qualities needed in the world today (healing, nurturing, rhythmic qualities) – if we are more awake to the life of feeling and imagination, more sensitive to the life of the heart, then perhaps we are called upon to recognise and develop these capacities and bring them into the life of our times. In large and small ways we can work to enliven the feeling life and warm the thinking life around us. If we truly attend to and foster our connections with each other, nature, and the cosmos, we will be able to encourage the awakening to the spirit in all human beings today. In knowing how to follow the spirit, we can help lead the way back to the spirit. Recovering and transforming our own capacity for maternal love, we can give this out to nourish all of humanity.

The poet, Rainer Maria Rilke, recognised this great task – the spiritualisation of the love relationship – in women's general awakening that he saw in his lifetime. In one of his *Letters to a Young Poet*, he writes:

"We are only just now beginning to look upon the relation of one individual person to a second individual objectively and without prejudice, and our attempts to live such associations have no model before them. And yet in the changes brought about by time there is already a good deal that would help our timorous novitiate.

"The girl and the woman, in their new, their own unfolding, will but in passing be imitators of masculine ways, good and bad, and repeaters of masculine professions. After the uncertainty of such transitions it will become apparent that women were only going through the profusion and the vicissitude of those (often ridiculous) disguises in order to cleanse their own most characteristic nature of the distorting influence of the other sex. Women, in whom life lingers and dwells more immediately, more fruitfully, and more confidently, must surely have become fundamentally riper people, more human people than easy-going man, who is not pulled down below the surface of life by the weight of any fruit of his body, and who, presumptuous and hasty, undervalues what he thinks he loves. This humanity of women, born in its full time in suffering and humiliation, will come to light when she will have stripped off the conventions of mere femininity in the mutations of her outward status, and those men who do not yet feel it approaching today will be surprised and struck by it. Some day (and for this, particularly in the northern countries, reliable signs are already speaking and shining), some day there will be girls and women whose name will no longer signify merely an opposite of the masculine, but something in itself, something that makes one think, not of any complement and limit, but only of life and existence: the feminine human being.

"This advance will (at first much against the will of the outstripped men) change the love experience, which is now full of error, will alter it from the ground up, reshape it into a relation that is meant to be of one human being to another, no longer of man to woman. And this more human love (that will fulfil itself, infinitely considerate and gentle, and kind and clear in binding and releasing) will resemble that which we are preparing with struggle and toil, the love that consists in this, the two solitudes protect and border and salute each other."[52]

Today there are many situations that might make us wonder if women are not still caught in being "imitators of the masculine", rather than finding their own real contribution to make to the life around them. Many women have stepped into traditional male, high-powered work situations on the old terms. They have taken on roles and positions of power that men are even beginning to find restrictive, and there is now an increasing incidence of stress-related diseases among women. Numbers of women have also become involved in activities that require a hardening and densifying of their physical bodies, i.e. mining, the army, body-building. Of course, the choice of occupation or activity is essentially an individual question and needs to be respected and understood as such. But there are also other signs that women in many different ways are waking up to the particular offering they have to make to the world today. They begin to uncover their own deeper values, and to find the courage to live and act from them.

They are finding the strength to resist, if necessary, the old ways of doing things, and to search for new ways of working together. They want to contribute to the world, not as men but as women, and they have a growing confidence in themselves and their experience. Some women today even choose to remain single, not for negative or reactive reasons, but because they recognise that they have a particular task in the world today. They know it is no longer enough for women to care for their personal relationships and family and the small circles of life around them; they now have a responsibility to bring their values and capacities into the larger world around them. Perhaps single women have a particular task and responsibility for the flow of the feminine into the works and ways of the larger world, for they have a greater amount of free energy than their sisters who have children and families to care for.

There is growing evidence that women bring a calming, civilising influence into the tougher, potentially violent jobs such as police work, and that where women work the atmosphere is better and the relationships between people more caring and harmonious. Women allow for more honesty and directness; they say what they think and do not so easily play games. They may bring a flexibility to their work situations and they demontrate an ability to carry the whole without getting fixed in one particular aspect. Thus they begin to foster a new social awareness. There are a growing number of women in influential positions – as government ministers, doctors, journalists – who speak of how they want to resist the temptation to manipulate people – to get a good story, to get someone's vote or money, to get results. They are committed to openness with people they work with, and they often seem able to loosen or dissolve the old, rigid, hierarchical working patterns. Because of the attention they are willing to give to their relationships and their concern for the welfare of the people around them, they are often respected and loved by their employees.

Our Search for Wholeness

Of course it is not only women who are attempting to find new ways of working together, new meaning and values which can flow into life. Women may have a special responsibility towards the renewal of the feminine in our lives – to act as midwives to the new living and balanced consciousness that is wanting to be born, to make a space for its conception, and to hold a vision for its future unfolding. But finally, both women and men need to work together to bring a new warmth and wholeness into life, to find a living imagination of the human being. They need to find the realm of soul where we all potentially can find wholeness. "For the soul is simultaneously male and female. It carries those two natures in itself. Its male element is related to what is called will, its female element to what is called imagination. . . Thus it comes about that the two sexed male/female soul inhabits a single sexed male or female body. . . The double sexedness of man is retired from the external world, where it existed in the pre-Lemurian period, into his interior. One can see that the higher inner essence of a human being has nothing to do with man or woman."[53]

So in the soul realm, we are already one, yet paradoxically this balance is a potential which depends on our inner work if it is actually to be realised. We need to find a way to bring both feminine and masculine together, to find the forces within us to create wholeness.

This search is fundamental to the rise of the Women's Movement in this century. I wrote earlier of how, in our far distant past after the division of the sexes, girls were educated to develop their imaginative facilities, and boys were educated to develop their physical strength and willpower. Throughout history (with variations and exceptions), the education, tasks and roles of women and men were tied to their biological nature. Men were the doers, the initiators. They were the warriors and the conquerors, the achievers and providers. They penetrated the world with their intellect and their will. They were the interpreters of the world. Women, on the other hand, bore children and tended the hearth. They were the guardians of the heart and of the imaginative feeling life of the home. They cared for the religious and moral tone, the atmosphere of the home. They nurtured the physical and spiritual development of humanity; they told the stories and passed on the wisdom gathered through generations. They were awake to the wisdom working in the cosmos and in nature; they were

not, like men, the interpreters of the world, but more the interp
of the spirit.

These divisions were once meaningful and the different tasks
equally valuable. Gradually, however, these tasks became fixed, and
particularly women's roles came to be undervalued, limited and more
and more oppressive. Men took on a superiority in the affairs of the
world, while women were increasingly confined and gradually
excluded from the world. Unlike men, their future vocation was
supposed to be determined by their sex.

As this situation became increasingly intolerable for numbers of
women, the Feminist Movement arose at the end of the 19th century
to challenge it. Primarily, women demanded the right of all women
(and therefore also of all human beings) to determine what they could
or could not do according to their own abilities, not according to what
society or others dictated. Thus the Women's Movement was a
tremendous impulse for the self-realisation and freedom of both
women and men, for the recognition of the individually emerging
spirit in all. However varied its face, or hidden its call, I think that
basically the Women's Movement arose for and rested on a new
picture of the human being as a being with an inwardness of soul, with
a spiritual individuality which has the possibility to free itself both
from outer determining factors, such as family, race, nation and sex,
and the conventions, values and expectations associated with them,
and from inner compulsions and determining factors. Within the
Women's Movement has lived a picture of the human being as a free
spirit which can work towards wholeness.

So the Women's Movement challenged all the old ideas of what it is
to be a man or a woman. And as people have struggled to free
themselves from the dictates of the past, all the old roles and
definitions and traditions that once gave security and meaning, have
crumbled. We know that our physical bodies and roles do not express
the totality of who we are. We have experimented with different roles,
tried to include and develop different sides of ourselves, in order to
find out and express who is living behind the appearance, the garment
of sex, or the different roles that we wear. We want to meet each other
beyond all outer forms, and know the divine that lives in each one. We
want to find our path in life out of our true centre, not from outer
forms or conventions. We want to fill our roles in a new way, with new
meaning, bringing to whatever we do a consciousness of our essential
individuality. We want to find a way to bring to expression and

fruitful interaction both feminine and masculine qualities within, to find a way to control and direct these energies so that we can work towards a wholeness of soul.

I think that however far women's liberation still has to go today to become real, many restrictions and barriers to that liberation have been lifted; there are various possible ways for women to find personal fulfilment and a voice in the world. Encouraged by the greater education and work possibilities and by the general consciousness-raising of the Women's Movement, women have developed a growing sense of their individuality. They have learned to acknowledge and express the more masculine sides of themselves, their intellect and will. They have learned that, together with men, they can achieve, provide, control and guide, that they can work with and in the material world, that they can express their creative energies in the world as well as in the home. Women today work in a variety of fields and professions, and motherhood has become a question of choice and consciousness. We no longer automatically fall into the role of wife, mother, or career-woman. We can still choose to serve, as we have done traditionally – we can be midwives, social workers, teachers or mothers, but we can also be pilots, plumbers or politicians. Of course, as I have already mentioned, we need to ask how real these freedoms are if women are denying real parts of themselves, or are becoming slaves to the world in the pursuit of material success. But as women find themselves and their own true inner meaning, they have the possibility of developing and expressing their humanity in whatever work they choose to do.

There have also been changes for men, especially in the last 20 years as a result of the renewed Women's Movement. As women have questioned the roles given them by society, men also have been able to free themselves from their role as chief breadwinner, worldly achiever and provider; they have begun to step back and look at their values. Many men have begun to seek a more meaningful work and lifestyle, one that will allow them to express more of their inner, imaginative life. As one man expressed it: "I do not want to get a heart attack for lack of a heart life". So more men express their willingness to give up their single minded pursuit of fame and worldly success, to spend more time with their wives and families. As men actually do spend more time in the home and do not just provide the material satisfactions or the discipline in the family, but actually play with and care for their children, the myth that men cannot nurture begins to break down. We realise that men also can be good parents, that they are also capable of love, intimacy and tenderness. There are many men today who make radical changes in their jobs in order to make this possible. Several years ago in *The Guardian* there was an interview with a solicitor who gave up his job and moved with his family into a smallholding in the country. The article began:

"Michael Tracy fulfilled the dream of many a professional Englishman when he escaped from a busy solicitor's practice in Worksop to till the soil in Donegal, Ireland. . . Financially he could not afford to leave his practice, but spiritually he could not afford to stay. 'I came to get away from a terrible way of life. I was working sometimes from 4 in the morning to 8 at night to make money we did not need. At the weekend there would be as many as 60 phone calls. I never saw the children. . . The trouble was that I never mastered the job. It mastered me, and took over my whole life.'"[54]

In *The Second Stage* Betty Friedan interviews many men with similar feelings and dilemmas. They express their growing unwillingness to live for money, or to live just for a job or for a company; they want to live for themselves, to have a creative family life. Yet these longings in them also make them feel uncertain and vulnerable, as all the traditional values and expectations surrounding what men should do collapse. This is captured in the following interview: "A hotshot MBA in Chicago baulks at the constant travelling, and the constant 60-80 hour week he is expected to work . . 'I'm supposed to leave Sunday night and get back Friday. My wife and I are getting to be strangers. Besides, I want to have a family. There are other things I want in life besides getting ahead in this company. But how can I say I won't travel like that when the other guys are willing to? They'll get ahead and I won't. How can I live for myself, and not just for the company?'"[55]

Growing unemployment has also contributed to the questioning men are involved in today about the meaning of being a man. It has begun to force them not only to redefine work but to find ways of defining themselves apart from their work. It has made them question the worth and meaning of outer recognition, status, and material prosperity when, from one day to the next, it can fall away. An article by Tom Crabtree called *Cheers to the Men of Tomorrow* looks at the challenges and opportunities unemployment could bring to men by making it a kind of necessity that they develop a more feminine side of themselves. The article starts:

"In years to come, a man will be judged more by who he is than by what he does, and he will need more skills to cope. So, come on, chaps – start living."

In the article Crabtree speaks about how, through the pain, misery and despair of unemployment, a new kind of man may arise who will be required to give up the macho, stiff upper lip, perfect and independent image and will have to learn to care and share, express his feelings and reach out to others. He will begin to see that work may not be just what you get paid for, but what you devote your energy to and that will need to include relationship and love, friendship and family as well as any outer work. Crabtree says:

"What you do is not what you are. Who you are is your secret self, how you relate to other people, and the courage you show in the face of real disappointment and pain. Given that macho man – in an age of electronics – is doomed, and given that we'll need sensitivity and intelligence (rather than biceps) to get through the next 20 years, here are a few tips for men which may help them face up to the future."[56]

Crabtree advises men not to give all they have to their jobs, to learn to listen rather than to speak, to learn to make themselves vulnerable and open, to recognise their interdependence with others. He says that they need to develop an interest in life questions, in the arts, and in others. So this article seems to point to a process which, I think, many men, either on their own, with other men, in men's groups, or with women have begun – the recognition and development of the feminine sides of themselves. Hopefully this inner work will also make possible the redemption and transformation of the masculine in our culture.

So, as our old roles and inflexible attitudes to them break down, as we try now to develop in ourselves what we previously left to the other, we increase the range and quality of our experience. Both women and men can develop imagination and will, the feminine and masculine sides of themselves. We have access to parts of ourselves that we previously left the other to develop. We become inwardly more mobile and begin to be able to change roles without fixing each other in those roles.

Through this, new kinds of relationships also become possible – not relationships of mutual dependency, but relationships of mutual development in which we are committed to growth and wholeness. As we drop our roles, the real possibility of relationship begins, the relationship of one self to another. As we develop ourselves and find a completeness within, selfless love becomes possible, a free giving of one individual to another. We begin to have an inkling of how we might carry the other without imposing or possessing. Yet we also need each other in order to develop. We are not finally separate but live within each other, and can hold for each other a picture of the higher self, of what is most longed for. So our search for individual balance is not separate from our learning to care for our relationships, and love becomes the ultimate wholeness we work towards today with the freedom and consciousness we have found through our separateness.

Of course, this is not as easy as it sounds. The media – films, advertising, etc, still feed us with stereotyped images of what a man or woman is. Intelligent women are sexless, business women are hard and cold, housewives are dumb. Men with aprons cleaning the kitchen are weak and silly, but behind cars they are powerful. A friend who got married in California only a few years ago received with her marriage licence a gift – a bottle of washing-up liquid, a packet of laundry detergent, a box of tampons and a novel called *Savage Passion*. Her comment was: "I guess the company that distributes these has a pretty narrow view of what brides do."

However, more to the point is that we ourselves are not as clear inwardly as we think. We struggle in our relationships without the security and certainty that the old roles gave us. The more traditional expectations lie deep and do not just disappear when we become more conscious of them. They tend to come up when we least expect them, and they need to be faced and worked through in any ongoing relationship. For instance, a man may feel very threatened by a woman's development, especially if she is his wife, but even if she is his colleague or friend. He may worry if she enters his sphere of work – will she be better at her work than he is –will she gain more recognition and acclaim? He may be worried if she becomes more qualified than he is, with more or better degrees. Similarly, a woman may feel uneasy if her partner starts taking responsibility in her traditional sphere of work – the home, the care of the children. She may want it, but feel uneasy if he turns out to be good at it. Whenever my youngest daughter became ill and both my husband and I had a class to teach, we would discuss who should stay at home that day. My daughter would say, "I hope it's Daddy because he plays with me".

That always made me feel inadequate, as though my husband was better at mothering than I was. I might have wanted to go and teach my class, but I wanted my daughter to want me. Of course, both men and women also feel guilty if they are not fulfilling the role expected of them, even if they have consciously chosen to do something else. The pressures from outside to conform are enormous, and these conspire with the hidden pressures within us.

Also, as we try to develop different sides of ourselves we need to acquire new skills, whether it is changing a tyre, baking a cake, changing a plug or changing a baby's nappy, for these outer capacities help to broaden our inner experience and give us confidence in the different spheres of life. What is our attitude towards the efforts of the other? Do we mock and laugh at the other's attempts? Or, can we learn to help each other and then step back and let them do things their way and not make them feel silly or ridiculous, so that we can truly build a shared life together. I was struck by Betty Friedan's chapter on "Women at West Point" in *The Second Stage*. The women were ridiculed and laughed at by men because they could not do the same physical exercises as the men. Yet it seems that many men could not meet the physical requirements 'to the letter' either, and that these standards had little relationship to what actually made a good officer. In their own way, women could manage the training well, and even had higher leadership ratings when it came to their ability to deal with and motivate the people they had to lead.

Perhaps the greatest obstacle to the achievement of true inner and outer balance, and the freedom and flexibility in the roles we wear, is still the undervaluing of the feminine, and the more feminine roles of serving others and caring for human relationships. We continue to think that real work is making money and acquiring material possessions and outer recognition. We overvalue what we can see, and measure and possess, the physical products of the intellect and the will. There are signs today that men are withdrawing from positions of power, from the 'rat-race', from the world of competition, manipulation, and hierarchy, into more creative and nurturing roles.

But, as men have stepped out, women have stepped in, leaving less time to care for themselves or others. There are signs of weariness, of stress-related illness, of brittleness among these women who had to fight their way into a male-dominated world. So clearly this in itself is no advance – a situation of role-reversal, where men and women take on the roles that the other found restrictive, merely repeating the old value system without a change in consciousness and understanding. Surely, behind and deeper than the question of the particular role we take on, lives the necessity of finding a new insight into human life, of creating an education for life – for both children and adults. This would foster an understanding of human development and the meaning of relationships, the meaning of being a mother or a father, and encourage us to begin to create a new family culture. When we begin to temper the values of competition, efficiency, production and quantity with more attention to cooperation, relationship, process and quality, when we value our social relationships as well as our economic and political life, and understand that the small circle of family is a kind of heart for the wider circle of our world and our universe, then we can begin to make real and responsible choices about how we live our lives. We can find individual ways to live and work together towards self-development and love, valuing both masculine and feminine qualities and bringing both together to express the wholeness of human experience.

This balance and freedom is not really found in our outer circumstances – certainly not in our physical bodies or even in the roles that we wear. We find ourselves, men or women, in a certain family and nation with a particular heredity. That is the material we have to work with and, working with, can free ourselves from. It is our self, our individuality, which incarnates throughout time taking turn after turn as a woman or man, that can work to free us from these outer circumstances, definitions and restrictions, and can control, direct and finally transform the qualities of feminine and masculine within. Thus, with this third force, the ego force within us, we can work consciously towards inner union; we can move beyond sex to express our full humanity, calling on whatever quality we need in the moment in order to be creative in what we do. It is this harmonising force that we can call on if we are caught in an overly critical stance and want to bring some warmth to the situation, or if we are swamped by our emotions and want to step back and bring more objectivity to our view.

So more important than how we arrange our lives or the particular role that we wear at the moment, is our capacity to remain flexible, to take on a role without fixing ourselves in it, seeing what is needed in the moment and bringing to whatever we do a consciousness of our free being, and a love for what we are doing. Then whatever we do is not a limitation but an expansion, for we can find in each task or situation an opportunity for growth and creativity, which needs a meeting and flow between the masculine and feminine sides of ourselves. We need to be both open and discriminating, warm and clear, flexible and firm. We need to nurture and to guide, to serve and to develop ourselves. We need a flow between our intellect and our imagination, our reason and our fantasy, our practical abilities and our intuition. We need to be dreamers and still keep our feet on the ground, to move between order and chaos, form and spontaneity. We need to find ways to actively nurture, to work consciously with rhythm, to join both head and heart, mind and body, spirit and matter; we need to know when and how to speak or listen, to act or wait. It has been suggested that we not only have a 28 day cycle for conception but also for concepts, that all people have a rhythm of 14 days receptive and 14 days productive and creative. If so, this would reflect the connection between sex and thinking, between the conception of a child and the conception of a thought. As we strive to bring the feminine and masculine principles within us to balance, we become inwardly fertile; we come to know ourselves and conceive our higher human self. And as we work to balance ourselves, we plant seeds of future balance for all humanity.

The Conception of Life

Many of the questions and dilemmas that we face challenge us to renew the feminine quality in our lives – to awaken our heart's vision, and work for a living understanding that will renew our imagination of the earth and of human beings. The growing interference in the sphere of conception through the development of technology and medical science is one place where this need for insight is particularly obvious and pressing. Here we are faced directly with the questions: What is our conception of life? How do we conceive children? and also how do we conceive of life itself?

It is important to try to look at and understand these developments without morally judging those who, in their longing for a child, find their only hope in in vitro fertilisation. It is probably too early still to judge the physical, psychological or spiritual consequences of this development, and I am sure that it is naive to think it will be stopped or that humanity will not be able to bear it. I think it is here to stay and it is now a question of how we meet it and work with it.

When I was growing up, Huxley's 'brave new world' of test-tube babies seemed far away, a fantastic story that would never be. I believed the biologist James Watson's prophecy that if we tampered in this area "all hell would break loose". Yet six years ago when the first test-tube baby was born, the world took it in its stride, and this new 'benefit' of modern medical science was greeted with enthusiasm. Not many questions were asked. Since then it has been described as 'a growing business'. There have been hundreds of babies born in this way, and the technical expertise has improved. But there is also now a growing concern about the moral implications of this development. People have begun to feel that science and technology are running ahead of morality; they wonder whether we face the spectre of supermarkets of embryos, labelled with sex and physical characteristics, guaranteed free of genetic defect.

So, many questions are now being asked, questions such as: When does life begin? Can we experiment on it and dispose of it at will? What is the permitted degree of imperfection? Can we allow commercial surrogacy – women carrying and giving birth to children for other women? In response to these and other questions, several groups were appointed to meet together to work out guidelines and controls for this new method of conception and the research connected with it. Basically a 'go-ahead' has been given to the research necessary for the technique of in vitro fertilisation to develop, and to the method itself. Freezing and storing of eggs, sperm and embryos, experimenting on embryos up to 14 or 17 days old, implanting donated embryos into women – all have been sanctioned. Only commercial surrogacy has been banned. The actual legal situation of this whole method of birth and research is still unclear, as various groups for or against surrogacy or experimentation on embryos battle each other to get their position legalised. Through this debate, however, many people are waking up to the fundamental issues involved and are beginning to question, and this is certainly positive.

I think it is important in considering this development to be clear about the lie that lives behind it – that this technique was developed for the benefit of infertile mothers. It seems that experiments to do with test-tube fertilised eggs were common from the 1950s, but to begin with in connection with research into contraception, not conception. Writing on this theme, Dr Thomas Weihs says that "by the early 1960s implantations of in vitro fertilised cells were performed in women, usually without their knowledge, who were to have gynaecological operations. The final 'achievement', therefore, is the result of a great deal of ethically very problematic research."[57] Dr Weihs also points out that other methods of relieving infertility are still more successful than in vitro fertilisation, so the special attraction of this method seems to lie more in its spectacular nature, in its revelation of the skills and ingenuity of modern medical science.

As this method becomes more widespread, the suffering of the women involved also becomes clear. Many relationships are strained and the expense grows enormous as women have to return over and over again to the clinics, swinging from hope to despair, facing one disappointment after another; they often have to try many times before conceiving and, after many attempts, they may still not conceive at all. So it appears that in the whole development of this technique the human suffering and human consequences have taken second place to the advancement of medical science.

However difficult the question, it is also important to ask if failure to conceive is only physical? I know how great the suffering of women and men can be who are unable to have children, and I do not mean that we should not search for ways to help their situation. But is the solution to further materialize the process of conception, or should we not try instead to find and work with the causes of infertility, which seem in part to be connected with the rise of venereal disease, abortion, and the use of the contraceptive pill. Beyond this, can we not try to foster a deeper questioning and work with the idea that what happens to us has meaning and is part of our continual becoming? Perhaps the inabiliy to have children may have a meaning for a person's growth and life tasks. There is a connection between our creative energies and our reproductive energies. There are also many places where creative, nurturing, maternal forces are needed today. Is it possible, then, for a woman to ask if there is another task for her besides having children? Do we always need to manipulate and control our lives, or can we try to understand and find meaning in the situations that meet us.

What really is the picture of the human being and conception on which this method is based? Is conception just a physical, technical event, or is it a spiritually creative act? Do we make babies – or create a space for the incarnation of a spiritual being? And, if we are more than our physical, material bodies, does it matter that our first home on earth is a test-tube rather than the warmth sphere of the mother's womb?

The phase of embryological development interfered with is minute compared with the whole development; it is the first few days of the first phase. But we know from Rudolf Steiner that at the moment of conception, when biologically the male and female cells meet and there is a 'cell death', a momentary breakdown of order, a chaos within the cell, there is a meeting of spirit with matter; the spirit germ, the archetypal human form, the image of God in which we are made, unites with the fertilized egg. After that, in this early phase, the embryo does not develop but waits while a home and environment is created. But if it is true what Karl König suggests in his lectures on *Embryology and World Evolution* – that the mother is a representative of the spiritual powers on earth, and that her whole reproductive cycle recapitulates cosmic evolution – what does it mean for an incarnating child to be separated from the mother and this re-enactment of cosmic evolution – even for a few days? We also know from Steiner that it is not until the 16th or 18th day after conception that the human individuality, enfolded in the astral etheric organisation, connects with the embryonic sheaths. This is the time that the human form first appears, when we can see the first sign of the head and spinal column. It is interesting that so far most guidelines given for embryo research have pointed to this time as the limit, beyond which experiments on embryos should not be allowed. There seems to be an unconscious awareness and reverence for the great spiritual drama being enacted at this moment.

So what is the meaning of this development in our time? Are we tampering with the divine creative process without purity and heart wisdom? What kind of response can we make towards this development? Already photographs and films of embryological development that are a kind of by-product of this research have awakened in people a sense of awe and wonder at the mystery of human development, a sense for the spiritual dimension of the process of conception and growth of human beings. So perhaps this development can stimulate us to ask ourselves – what is a human being? What is conception? What is the meaning of having a child? Or a relationship? Perhaps it will encourage us to search for an insight and understanding of life that includes the spiritual and to work for a capacity to listen into this realm; to listen across the threshold to the unborn, and to what is wanting to be born in us and through us, and in others. I think that through the development of new inner capacities of understanding that can then work creatively into our relationships with others, and help us to make our lives artistic and meaningful, we will find ways to meet and redeem the technological manipulation of life that confronts us today. By working inwardly, we will be able to find a true conception of life and bring it into life.

Connected with the manipulation of birth and the interference of the whole middle realm of the heart is the growth of the contraceptive industry, especially the development of the birth control pill which, while giving women the illusion of freedom, is in many ways further enslaving her, cutting her off not only from her bodily rhythms and well-being, but also from her maternal and nurturing capacities, her deepest sense of self and connection with the spirit.

The dilemmas that surround birth control and woman's traditional role as nurturer and sustainer of life are highlighted by the question of abortion. This is a heart-rending question that calls us to look at our conception of life, death and the human being. Its close relation to the questions of manipulated conception is underlined by the fact that money from legal abortions was used to fund test-tube baby research. Like the question of in vitro fertilisation, there are no easy, straightforward answers to this growing phenomenon, and it is certainly not a question of any conventional right or wrong. But this, and the suffering involved, need not keep us from trying to understand what is happening. Only if we look honestly and openly, with compassion for the human situation and insight into the spiritual dimensions, can we take responsibility for our actions.

It is important that women have gained the right to choose to have an abortion or not, but in the fight for this right, abortion has become a political issue and this has polarized people into those "for abortion" and those "for life". But who is only for abortion, and what does pro-life mean when "pro-lifers" bomb abortion clinics in the USA? The polarization and political fight only cloud the real issue, for surely abortion is essentially an individual, moral question. By making it a legal question we take responsibility away from women, to whom it really belongs, and give it to the law-makers; we are tempted to act from an abstract idea rather than from understanding or intuition. Of course it is a question that has to do with men too; indeed all of humanity share in the responsibility for abortion.

Sex is to do with the Biblical fall, with the whole karma of the earth and human beings as physical, sexual beings. It is where we are most vulnerable. In the Bible no one was free enough of 'sin' to stone the woman taken in adultery – nor did Christ condemn her but instead he wrote her deed into the earth. It belonged to the destiny of the earth. Sexual errors are somehow carried by all of us and the situation today is surely the result of how any and all of us think about sex, reproduction, the meaning of having a child, the meaning of relationships, of life and death, and the conception of life that lives in our daily thoughts and deeds. Yet in the end, abortion is often a very lonely choice for women. They are often pressurized by doctors, counsellors, their families, or the father – regardless of whether the heart prompts them to have the child. Thousands of women have wrestled with this question and we have a responsibility to wake up to what we are doing.

What does it mean to cut off the relationship intended by the conception of a new life? There is a growing awareness that relationships continue after death. Indeed, more women are aware of the presence of the unborn and can sense the being of the child that is wanting to be born to them, its longing to come to earth. Perhaps we need to recognise and be more aware of this realm of the unborn. But it is also helpful for many women who carry a burden of grief and guilt about abortion to realize that externally terminating a relationship does not end it – that it will find its form and transformation in time. The problem of abortion was highlighted for me by a letter to a national newspaper several years ago from a woman who had three

children and, through an IUD failure found that she was pregnant
again. She truly believed that the world was overpopulated and that
she had her "fair share of children". She thought that to have an
abortion was the morally right thing to do, and in this thought she
was supported by her friends. Afterwards no one could understand
her suffering, her grief, and her sense of loss. In her letter she said
that she thought that every woman had the right to choose, but that
our free choice was more terrible than we realised. She asked where
"the latter-day humanist" was to seek for moral guidance? Realising
that she had acted out of an abstraction rather than the promptings
of her heart, she said that in retrospect it would have been wiser to
follow her heart rather than her reason.

Our heart is our guide to the many questions asking us to find a
new, fuller conception of life today. In the sometimes terrible choices
that we have to make lie the seeds of a new, truly human action. But
also in the seemingly smaller and less dramatic situations of our lives
there are many opportunities for us to begin to awaken a centre in
ourselves out of which can flow true human understanding and love,
bringing a new warmth and wholeness into our lives.

Phases of Life

Each individual's life from conception to old age also moves towards wholeness. I want to give a brief and general picture of this development, as it adds another dimension to our struggle for balance if we understand that each phase of our life brings a possibility to uncover and integrate a different aspect of ourselves.

We all begin in the androgynous round of the womb, a state of unconscious union similar to the mythological state of oneness, of humanity's beginning, the great cosmic egg in which all opposites are contained and joined, the fluid state of original androgyny where female and male are undivided. The developing embryo recapitulates the original coming into being of humanity and we all carry this memory deep within us. At the moment of conception, the spirit germ which is neither male nor female but both male and female, unites with the physical germ. At the foundation of our individual beginnings then is the primal human form, the celestial and androgynous Adam.

The oneness of our beginnings has a feminine direction. Although genetic sex is established at conception, for the first five or six weeks of its development an embryo is morphologically female. This femaleness of our beginnings in the womb echoes the picture that Rudolf Steiner gives of the original androgynous human beings who were both female and male, and yet in their physical form approximated that of the female.

In early infancy and childhood we still live in the feminine round. An infant is a pure being, existing in a state of divine union before separation or division. In the early weeks of a child's life more divinity than humanity shines through its eyes. Infancy is a time of sleep, when consciousness is open and receptive. It is a moon time, a time of sensation and imitation, rhythm and stability, a time of nourishment, protection, caring and comfort. Children mirror their surroundings; the environment impresses itself upon them because they feel one with it. The young child feels one with its mother and its environment; mother and child, inner and outer, the moral and the physical are one. For children then the world is still alive with being (they say hello and goodbye to houses, stones and trees as well as to people). Children move with a flexibility and ease between the opposites. They are not fixed in their sex but retain something of the oneness of our original androgynous nature. Although the germ cells are developed by the age of five, they wait another ten years or so before they function properly; this allows the free development of the imaginative, moral life. Thus the time of early childhood in many ways mirrors the prehistorical matriarchal time of goddess worship when human beings experienced a dream-like, imaginative consciousness, and felt themselves to be a part of the oneness of all things.

However, quite early on in childhood there are also signs of differentiation and of the awakening of the sense of individuality. The masculine principle begins to emerge. Babies' fontanelles close, their bodies gradually lose their softness and grow firmer, longer and more proportional; they stand up and learn to walk and talk; they gradually move from the circle to uprightness and thereby acquire a new independence.

Around the age of three, they say 'I' and begin to experience a first separateness from the world. Around the age of five, a new and dim consciousness of self appears and individual memory begins to develop.

In the years between seven and fourteen, when children go to school and become increasingly involved in the world outside the home, they begin to feel different and separate from their family and the small circle that has held and nurtured them until now. At seven they are still more or less one with the world around them, but by the age of nine they have taken a step back and differentiated themselves more from their environment. Around this time they have a strong sense of their own individuality and their feeling of separation from the world can be so profound that they may even think they have been adopted. They may challenge: "Are you my real mother?" They may also experience a heightened awareness and fear of death. They begin to form judgments and are concerned with rules, obedience and authority. They often create their own exacting moral codes; and their games are filled with rules which they enforce strictly. They are interested in limits and what is or is not out of bounds. This setting of boundaries connects to the time in creation myths when day and night, heaven and earth, male and female, are divided and the masculine principle emerges.

Between the ages of seven and fourteen children need less free play and more discipline and guidance. They need to find an authority to revere and follow. They begin to want to learn and express themselves. As they learn to read and write and count, they gradually move out of the world of pictures into abstraction, out of the dream, the imaginative consciousness into the world of intellect and material reality, from the feminine to the masculine. Throughout the middle years of childhood, seven to fourteen, children are artists, living in their feeling life, experiencing strongly goodness or badness, beauty and ugliness, sadness or happiness. Although they are no longer one with nature, nature is nevertheless experienced as alive. By the end of this phase, however, children's intellects awaken and they take yet another step back from the world. Nature becomes knowable and children become interested in observing the outer phenomenon in a more detached and objective way. They move from artist to scientist. They leave the Garden of Eden and enter the world.

At puberty when they fall into division, into their one-sexed bodies, their capacity for intellectual thinking and independent judgment awakens, and begins to develop. Concepts and ideas and the search for truth become important. Personality begins to unfold as they struggle to find independence, their own identity and authority and an understanding of the world. The time of puberty reflects the time of the division of the sexes when the capacity for thought and the entry of the spirit into human beings was linked with the formation of female and male physical bodies. With the division of the sexes, and the experience of that event in puberty, the longing for knowledge and the capacity for self-consciousness awakens. We are able to conceive babies and thoughts. Connected with our awakening sexuality is a ripening for love – an ever-widening interest in others and the world.

Rudolf Steiner speaks of how in ancient times puberty was a soul process as well as a physical process. People knew that when the "sexual essences" entered them the "divine was then pouring itself forth within."[58] They felt that at puberty the true human being entered. Sex and reproduction were connected with the divine order of things, with the microcosm-macrocosm bond of humanity.

"The boy of fourteen or fifteen years old experienced not only that his voice changed, but that what today only enters, presses into, the region of the voice, extending from the sexual essences of the organism, in those ancient times pressed also into the thoughts, the conceptual world of the young boy . . . Today the voice breaks; in those days the thoughts 'broke' too, since it was still the ancient imaginative time . . . Both sexes, only in different ways, experienced the fact that they actually knew in the soul: In me something is born which cosmic space has fructified in me."[59]

Ancient puberty rites seem to have been concerned with helping young people entering the adult community to understand the connection between microcosm and macrocosm, between the knowledge process and the cosmos. The young person was encouraged to reflect on the connection between human mortality and human reproduction. They were led to see how individuals in their development live through what was once the destiny of humanity. In many primitive puberty rites, people often performed symbolic acts of wholeness. For example, girls dressed as boys or boys dressed as girls. It may be that living behind this kind of ritual was an understanding that one would be a better, fuller adult woman or man if one was first a totality, if one re-enacted and reflected on one's original perfection. Perhaps too in such activities lived an awareness that the path of differentiation and separation eventually leads back to wholeness, for if we truly come to know our individuality we will become universal.

So at puberty young people begin to search for their sexual identity. Their development, the way they experience and relate to the world will be different. Generally boys will incline more towards the physical, material world, whereas girls will incline more towards the cosmos and the aesthetic sides of life. Obviously as boys and girls come to know themselves as women and men, there will be a certain imbalance of feminine and masculine energies. However, it is also important that girls and boys are allowed to remain flexible and open to both feminine and masculine ways of being, so that they do not become too one-sided. Girls may need to be encouraged to retain an interest in the world of facts, ideas and physical activities, while boys need to be helped to keep in touch with their more emotional, intuitive sides.

Already in adolescence the long quest to find our 'other half' begins. In early adolescence this may at first be expressed in a love for the same sex, perhaps a hero-worship or an idealisation of an older woman or man. The young person may first experience their inner femaleness or maleness strongly, and look for its complement and balance outside themselves. This is a normal part of one's development. Later as young people come more fully into their physical sexual identity they search for their opposite outside themselves in the love for a woman or a man. This is the beginning of the long quest to find our other half. At this time our search manifests particularly in the seeking of relationship with the opposite sex, but also within the developing, young adolescent girl or boy there stirs an unconscious longing for a true integration of the other half within and a new harmony of the feminine and masculine sides of their being.

From puberty to mid-life the sexes tend to polarise and people live most fully into their sexual roles. This is probably necessary for the unfolding of our personalities and individuality. But as we discover ourselves as women or men, we also need to know ourselves as full human beings. While life requires that roles and tasks are divided, we need to take care that outer divisions do not become inner ones, so that some people control, think and organise while others feel and harmonise.

In the twenties, as we gain greater self-confidence and begin to experience ourselves more strongly from within, we seek to experience the world and test this newly developing self against it. We want to discover ourselves, to try out our capacities, to develop our personality and begin to define ourselves mainly through our feelings towards others and the world around us. A woman may first define herself as a woman at this time, or when she has children. Certainly during this phase many women marry, have children and create a home, and thus express their more feminine sides, while men begin a career and let their masculine qualities unfold. But most women and men today cannot move into these traditional roles without a lot of questioning and struggle. They want to know where the space is for themselves? (Betty Staley deals with this at length in her section.)

If we do emphasise a particular side of ourselves in the twenties there will often be a reversal later. Whenever in our lives we become too one-sided we are in danger of losing touch with our humanity and the other side of ourselves will call out to be realised. If we heed this call, we can begin to work towards balance, making up for past deficiencies and developing in ourselves what we have left undeveloped. Often in the thirties or forties people come to a crisis point which challenges them to expand themselves.

Women generally meet this crisis earlier than men, in the years between 28 and 35, perhaps because women are less earthbound than men, and this is a time of coming down to earth, of awakening to the material and practical aspects of our lives. It can be a very masculine time – a time when our more logical thinking is in the forefront, when we develop a passion for rational truths. People in this phase of life are often concerned with planning, ordering, organising the details of their lives, finding a new school for the children, buying a home, buying filing cabinets, and generally taking on a new responsibility in their sphere of work. There can be a growing objectivity and detachment towards the world and concerns of life. It can also be a time when people find more of an inner equilibrium and grow more confident and secure. It is the age when men and women find and develop their work, create a family culture, and deepen their friendships. Still, for women, there is often a crisis. They may feel that their beauty is fading, that life has become mechanical and routine, lacking adventure and passion. They may have a sense of meaninglessness, and a fear of death may suddenly arise in them.

Both women and men may experience a kind of inner death in their early 30s, a sense of inner decline, a loss of all the old talents and possibilities. They may begin to look inward and find a need for a new inner working in order to become creative. Sometimes a woman who has had children and begins to feel a bit freer at this time, thinks about having another baby. It may be important, however, that she ask herself if she is wanting another physical child or rather if it is an inner child that she needs to bring to birth. Having another child may sometimes be a way of putting off the challenge of self-development and the moment of insecurity which can lead to the finding of a new task. However, it may truly be another child that is wanting to be born and at this age a woman may begin to take on her task as mother more consciously and professionally. Whatever we choose to do during this phase, we begin to move from a more instinctive way of doing and being into consciousness.

We try to integrate the various sides of ourselves in our twenties but in our thirties and forties we must begin to succeed. Women who have made homes and cared for their children usually begin to look for a new source of self-esteem. They want to find some new work or career; they may take up what they had put aside when their children were small. Women in this phase often find the opportunity to express the more masculine sides of themselves. Also, today, many women find that by the time they are in their thirties they are bringing up their children alone. Some women choose to do this, but most find themselves confronted by a situation they cannot easily handle and certainly would not have chosen. Men increasingly find themselves in a similar situation. Suddenly a women or a man must be both mother and father to their children. They may have a job as well as carrying the full responsibility for home and family. This crisis often forces a person to see that they have only developed half of themselves. Out of necessity, then, they begin to learn how to work out of both their feminine and masculine sides.

Women who have had careers do not escape the crisis in the the thirties, but for them the questions are different. Their more maternal sides often want to be expressed and they may wonder: "Should I have a baby? It's getting late!". Or they may suddenly want to create a real home for themselves, to relax their ambitions and goals a bit and allow their softer sides a chance to blossom. They may also begin to feel dissatisfied with the way they have approached their work and try to express their more feminine sides in their work situations. Betty Friedan interviewed many young working women facing this crisis. For example one women in her thirties who had just been promoted was quoted as saying: "I'm up against the clock, you might say. If I don't have a child now, it will be too late. But it's an agonising choice. I've been supporting my husband while he gets his Ph.D. We don't know what kind of job he'll be able to get. There's no pay when you take off to have a baby in my company. They don't guarantee you'll get your job back. If I don't have a baby,will I miss out on life somehow? Will I really be fulfilled as a woman?"[60]

Men also have to encounter and learn to express the other side of themselves, though this may become an inner necessity at a later age than it does for women, for their biology does not force the issue in the same way. But the men who have devoted their energies singlemindedly to their careers may, in the mid-thirties or early forties, begin to feel the meaninglessness and emptiness of their ambitions. They may begin to feel dissatisfied with their lives and become aware that they have neglected whole areas of themselves in their push for success, money and recognition. It is often their more feminine side that has been neglected and has remained dormant. Seeing this, many men will change jobs at this time, looking for some creative and meaningful task that will allow them to cultivate their more sensitive and imaginative sides. Businessmen may suddenly turn to the arts or a caring profession, such as social work. Many men suddenly want to spend more time with their families, to turn inwards and reflect. Relationships can potentially deepen and become more harmonious in this phase of life. As each person discovers and develops the other half within themselves, they can withdraw their projection from their partner and can begin to relate to the true being of the other out of their own individuality.

As we grow older, we have the opportunity if we have worked to integrate ourselves, to come to a conscious balance of the feminine and masculine within. Even our physical bodies reflect this possibility. As women and men grow older, hormonal changes shift the balance so that in some ways we can experience both poles of femaleness and maleness in our physical bodies. Women and men tend to become more alike, or less different, in old age. As men grow older, their male hormone level decreases while their bodies become less efficient at getting rid of any excess female hormones. Therefore in middle age their female hormone level begins to climb or at least remain stable, so that men are actually producing more female hormones. As their bodies grow rounder and softer, they begin to move towards the androgynous round of their beginnings. Gail Sheey writes in her book *Passages:* "As he moves into the 50s, the contours of his body generally regain some of the femaleness that was anatomically natural to the original embryo."[61]

A woman's situation is similar. Her male hormone level does not rise, but her female hormone level, especially that of oestrogen, declines. Women's bodies often become more linear and harder, and their voices may deepen. Of course, this is a general picture and there are obviously many exceptions – there are many round, old women, and bony, old men. But in old age there is a real movement towards inner union, towards the unisex of old age, and the physical changes that occur in women and men reflect this movement.

Usually in the late forties or early fifties women experience the menopause. This can be a very difficult time for women. They often experience a variety of distressing physical and related psychological symptoms which can be mild or quite severe. But depression and discomfort are not the only things that women experience at this time. Especially after the menopause, many women speak of having a new vitality and an enormous sense of freedom and well being. Perhaps if we can begin to free ourselves from our ties to our physical body at this time, if we can accept our physical decline positively and, at the same time, find an inner meaning and work, we will be able to live into the real possibilities of this phase of our lives. The connection between physical and spiritual fertility, between conception in the mind and conception of a child, suggests that as we become infertile physically we may be able to use our freed energy to become spiritually fertile. If, as Dr. König suggests, the menstrual cycle is a kind of spiritual memory, a recollection and re-enactment of the evolution of the earth, then perhaps with the cessation of menstruation, we are free of the past and begin to work towards a future. If the beginning of menstruation marks the time when the sexes divide, the time of puberty when we come fully into our sexual bodies, perhaps at menopause we have the opportunity to regain our dual-sexed nature and the wholeness that we lost in childhood. Perhaps we can use our released energy to renew ourselves, to come to a new blossoming out of an inner harmony. So women in old age have the possibility of becoming virgin again. I do not mean this in the restrictive modern sense, but in the way great goddesses were virgin, in the way the term has been used throughout the ages to mean wholeness, one in oneself, and union with the spirit.

In old age women and men have a potential to come in consciousness to wholeness and open again to the spirit. It is a time when we can give up our specific sexuality, assimilate our feminine and masculine sides, and come again to our original androgynous nature. If in our lives we have worked for balance, that balance begins to be a reality. If we can accept our physical down-going, we can discover a new source of life within ourselves. It is a time when we can turn inward and find ourselves and turn outwards again to the world, a time of both receptivity and penetration, of love and wisdom. Inner and outer, feminine and masculine, become one.

In our development through life we come full circle. In our end we find our beginning. My daughter's great-grandfather christened her just before he died, when he was 90 and she was 9 months. He said to her then: "You and I are almost the same age". The very young and the very old meet in their openness to the universe and their oneness with the spirit. They are both in the round; in the cycle of our existence birth and death meet. In the embryo and in early infancy we are androgynous. We fall out of this oneness in our development through life, but in old age we can come again to union, a union where we can be conscious of all aspects of ourselves instead of having them unconscious within us. "Thus the great round . . . arches over a man's life, encompassing his earliest childhood and receiving him again, in altered form, at the end."[62]

Historically we have not come so far. We have moved out of androgyny, and out of matriarchy, where consciousness was still one with the spirit, into differentiation and development of the masculine principle. The evolution of consciousness needed this differentiation. The division of the sexes was necessary for the development of our thinking and our freedom. Through the growth of the masculine and the suppression of the feminine we were guided out of that early dream consciousness into matter. But we have come to a time in history and our society when balance must be found, the kind of balance that is possible when a woman or man comes to old age rightly. The Bible gives us a picture of such a goal. It moves from Paradise, wholeness and androgyny, through expulsion from Paradise, and finally in the end to Heavenly Jerusalem, which is a picture of life's wholeness, of perfection regained in consciousness. And this heavenly city is seen in the image of a bride, the eternal feminine, the Sophia and her all embracing divine wisdom. "And I, John, saw the Holy City, New Jerusalem, coming down from God out of Heaven, prepared as a bride adorned for her husband."[63]

The feminine then is intimately connected with the state of wholeness, the reunification of the opposites towards which we strive. She initiates our recovery of wholeness and a full experience of our humanity. 'Man' was cast out of Paradise "lest he put forth his hand and take also from the Tree of Life, and eat and live forever". Today we have begun to tamper with the Tree of Life. We have the power of life and death in our hands. As we reach for immortality and try 'to become as gods' we are in danger of corrupting life and destroying ourselves and our possibilities for evolution. In order to avoid disaster, we must work for a conscious balance in ourselves and in society, for only when we have attained the enlightened union of the New Jerusalem can we truly find access to the Tree of Life.

The heavenly Jerusalem is made "according to the measure of a man, that is, of the angel." It is a human city, a city of the imagination, like the inward space we need to create for ourselves and our lives. We need to become receptive to our true spiritual nature, to make ourselves the bride adorned for her bridegroom. Then we may come to the union and balance we long for; we will know ourselves in the sense of being inwardly fertile and open to what meets us out of the cosmos. This is an ideal that we can work towards in ourselves, with others, and in the world. It is an ideal that requires renewal of the feminine in our lives. In the following passages from the poem *For Eleanor and Bill Monahan,* the American poet William Carlos Williams makes a beautiful and moving plea for this renewal. The poem is a kind of prayer of an old man who, in the round of old age, calls on the feminine principle for himself and for the whole of humanity. The poem begins, and is addressed to

"Mother of God! Our lady! . . .

You have no lovers now
     in the bare skies
         to bring you flowers,
to whisper to you
     under a hedge
         how be it.
You are young
     and fit to be loved.
         I declare it boldly
with my heart
     in my teeth
         and my knees knocking
together. Yet I declare
     it, and by God's word
         it is no lie. Make us
humble and obedient to His Rule . . .

The moon which
     they have vulgarised recently
         is still
your planet
     as was Dian's before
         you. What
do they think they will attain
     by their ships
         that death has not
already given
     them? Their ships
         should be directed
inward upon. . . But I
     am an old man. I
         have had enough.
The female principle of the world
     is my appeal
         in the extremity
to which I have come.
        O clemens! O pia! O dolcis!
        Maria! "[64]

Footnotes

1. Robert Duncan, *The Truth and Life of Myth, An Essay in Essential Autobiography*, The Sumac Press, Fremont, Michigan 1968, p.323.

2. William Blake, *Complete Writing* Ed. Geoffrey Keynes, "Jerusalem", Oxford University Press, London 1966, p.716.

3. Denise Levertov, *The Jacobs Ladder*, "The Thread", A New Directions Paperback, New York 1961, p.48.

4. *The Holy Bible*, King James Version, "The Revelation of St John the Divine" chapter 12, verse 1.

5. Paula Browne, "If in time to come" *The Anthroposophical Review*, Vol 7, No. 3, p.15.

6. Rudolf Steiner, *The Search for the New Isis, Divine Sophia*, 4 lectures, Dornach 23-26 December 1920.

7. HD, *Trilogy* "Tribute to Angels", Carcanet Press 1973, pp.97, 103-105.

8. Marie Louise von Franz, *The Problem of the Feminine in Fairy Tales*, The Analytical Psychology Club, Spring Publications, New York 1972.

9. Erich Neumann, *The Origins and History of Consciousness*, Princeton University Press, trans. from German by R. F. C. Hull, New Jersey 1973, p.10.

10. Fiona Macleod, *The Divine Adventure, Iona Studies in Spiritual History*, William Heinemann Ltd., London 1925. This is a writer who, because of the nature of his subject – Celtic and Gaelic sagas – wrote with a female pseudonym. His real name was William Sharp.

11. Robert Duncan, *Roots and Branches*, "Apprehensions" Charles Scribners and Sons, New York 1964, p.30.

12. Emil Bock, *Studies in the Gospels*, Letter XVIII, trans. Margaret Mitchell, ed. Martha Heimeran, Christian Community Bookshop, p.67.

13. Rudolf Steiner, *Cosmic Memory: Lemuria and Atlantis*, Steinerbooks, trans. Karle Zimmer, New York 1976, p.86.

14. Bock, p.63.

15. Rudolf Steiner, *Knowledge of the Higher Worlds and its Attainment*, Rudolf Steiner Press, London 1963, p.39.

16. Rudolf Steiner, *The Fifth Gospel.*

17. *The Holy Bible* "Genesis" chap. 3 verse 5-7.

18. Rudolf Steiner, *Egyptian Myths and Mysteries*, Lecture 9, Anthroposophic Press, New York 1971, p.92.

19. William Irving Thompson, *The Time Falling Bodies Take to Light; Mythology, Sexuality and the Origin of Culture*, St Martins Press, New York 1981, p.208.

20. Jean Paul Sartre, *Nausea*, trans. Robert Baldick, Penguin 1965.

21. Rudolf Steiner, *The Theosophy of the Rosicrucians*, Rudolf Steiner Press, London 1966, p.141.

22. *The Holy Bible* "Galatians" chap. 3 verse 18.

23. Ibid. "The Revelation of St John the Divine" chap. 1 verse 8.

24. William Blake, "Milton" Book Two in *Blake, Complete Writings* ed. Geoffrey Keynes, Oxford University Press, 1972, p.533.

25. Rudolf Steiner, *The Gospel of St John in Relation to the Other Gospels, especially that of St Luke*, lectures, Kassel, June 24 – July 7, 1909, trans. G. Mexta, Percy Lund Humphries & Co. Ltd., London, Lecture XI p.209.

26. *The Apocryphon of John* quoted by Elaine Pagels in "The Suppressed Gnostic Feminism" The New York Review, Nov. 22 1979.

27. *The Gospel according to Thomas*, Coptic Text, trans. by A. Guillaumont, H. Ch. Puech, G. Quispel, W. Till and T. Yassah 'Abd Al Masih, 1959, Leiden, E. J. Brill, Collins, London, p.17.

28. John Donne, "The Canonization" from *John Donne's Poems* ed. Hugh L'Anson Fausset, Everyman's Library, London, J. M. Dent & Sons Ltd, 1960, p.7.

29. Rudolf Steiner, *Mystery Centres and Mystery Knowledge.*

30. Steiner, *The Gospel of St John in Relation to the Other Gospels*, Kassel, p.210.

31. Dr Karl König, MD, *Embryology and World Evolution*, trans. R. E. K. Meuss FIL, reprinted from the British Homeopathic Journal, Lecture 2 October 15-16 1965, p.10.

32. Corinne Hunt, *Males and Females*, Penguin Education 1973, p.83.

33. See lecture by Dr König.

34. M. J. Sherfey, *The Nature and Evolution of Female Sexuality*, Vintage Books, New York, 1973, p.40,45.

35. Rudolf Steiner, *The Gospel of St Mark*, The Rudolf Steiner Publishing Co. London, 1947, Lecture 10, p.214.

36. Rudolf Steiner, *The Manifestations of Karma*, Rudolf Steiner Press, 1968, Lecture IX p.205.

37. Ibid.

38. Rudolf Steiner, *The Christ Impulse and the Development of Ego Consciousness*, The Anthroposophic Press, New York, 1976, p.102.

39. Rudolf Steiner, *Health and Illness*, Vol 2, The Anthroposophic Press, New York, p.56.

40. König, p.11.

41. Bernard Lievegoed, *Phases: Crisis and Development in the Individual*, Rudolf Steiner Press, London, 1979, trans. H. S. Lake.

42. Rudolf Steiner, *The Theology of the Rosicrucians*, Lecture II, Rudolf Steiner Press, London, p.23.

43. Ibid.

44. Rudolf Steiner, "Man and Woman in Light of Spiritual Science", *Anthroposophical Review* Vol 2, No. 1, pp.11-13.

45. Perhaps the qualities of devotion and inner courage that women often show come from their male etheric. Rudolf Steiner says that "a man becomes a warrior through the outer courage of his bodily nature, a woman possesses an inner courage, the courage of sacrifice and devotion. The man brings his creative activity to bear on external life. The woman works with devoted receptivity into the world." Ibid., p.11.

46. Steiner, *The Theosophy of the Rosicrucians*, p.56.

47. Steiner, *The Manifestations of Karma*, p.207.

48. Ibid., pp.204,207.

49. Robert Bly, *New Age* "What Men Really Want", May 1982, pp.30-51.

50. *Guardian Women* Interview "The Chains of Liberation" by Liz Forgan, London, May 25, 1978.

51. Betty Friedan, *The Second Stage*, Michael Joseph, London 1982, pp.26-27.

52. Rainer Maria Rilke, *Letters to a Young Poet*, trans. M. D. Herter Norton, W. W. Norton & Co., New York 1934, pp.58-59.

53. Steiner, *Cosmic Memory*, pp.88-91.

54. *The Guardian*.

55. Betty Friedan, p.43.

56. Tom Crabtree "Cheers to the Men of Tomorrow . . ."

57. *The Anthroposophical Review* Vol 2, No.1, "Test Tube Babies", Thomas Weihs MD, p.22.

58. Rudolf Steiner, *Ancient Myths, their Meaning and Connection with Evolution*, Lecture II, trans. M. Cotterell, Steiner Book Centre, Toronto, Canada, English edition 1971, p.22.

59. Ibid., p.20-21.

60. Betty Friedan, p.22.

61. Gail Sheehy, *Passages, Predictable Crises of Adult Life*, Dutton Books, New York, 1976, p.446.

62. Eric Neumann, p.37.

63. *The Holy Bible* "The Revelation of St John the Divine" chap. 21 verse 2.

64. William Carlos Williams, *Pictures from Brueghel and other poems*, New Directions 1962, "For Eleanor and Bill Monahan", pp.83-86.

205

Acknowledgements

Hawthorn Press wishes to thank Paula Browne and Sylvia Mehta for kind permission to use their poems and for their encouragement and moral support in this venture.

Our thanks also to Paul Matthews for his poem 'The Lady' which appears in *The Fabulous Names of Things* available at £1.50 from the author, Paul Matthews, Emerson College, Forest Row, Sussex.

Early versions in essay form of work which led to *Ariadne's Awakening* appeared in *The Anthroposophical Review* and *The Threshing Floor*.

'The Thread' by Denise Levertov, *Poems 1960 - 1967*, copyright 1961 Denise Levertov Goodman, 'Tribute to the Angels' by Hilda Doolittle, *Collected Poems 1912 - 1944*, copyright 1982 The Estate of Hilda Doolittle, 'For Eleanor and Bill Monahan' and 'Pictures from Brueghel' by W. C. Williams, copyright 1954 William Carlos Williams, are reproduced with permission from New Directions Publishing Corporation, U.S.A. and Carcanet New Press Ltd, Manchester, U.K.

The Authors

Signe Schaefer co-ordinates and teaches in the Orientation year at the Waldorf Institute in Spring Valley, New York. She is married with two children in their late teens. Signe helps with workshops relating to 'Ariadne' themes as well as working with biography. She was a contributor to the book *Lifeways*.

Betty Staley has taught for over twenty years in the Sacramento Waldorf School, is on the faculty of the new Rudolf Steiner College, and involved in teacher training. She has three children, and wrote the children's book *Ow and the Crystal Clear*. She has also written a book on adolescence soon due for publication in America.

Margli Matthews grew up in California but resides now in England where she teaches at Emerson College in Forest Row, Sussex. She is married with two teenage daughters. Margli was a contributor to *Lifeways*, and helps with group work and workshops on themes ranging from personal to wider social questions.

Social Ecology Series: In Print

DYING FORESTS a crisis in consciousness.
Transforming our way of life.
46 colour pictures and text by Jochen Bockemühl.
Introduction by Professor Brian Goodwin.
Translated by John Meeks.

Forests are dying in central Europe – many trees are dying in the Swiss mountains, threatening erosion problems. Many lakes in Scandinavia, Scotland and North Wales now have no fish. Sulphur dioxide, ozone, nitric oxides from industry, traffic and power stations are some causes. But what part do people play in causing forest die-back?

Dying Forests offers the insights of Jochen Bockemühl – both scientist and artist – into the underlying causes of forest die-back. These causes relate closely to our modern life style and our destructive forms of thinking and ways of exploiting nature. The author, by means of his water colour sketches and commentary, describes how, through the development of a sensitive observation of landscape ecology, a more conscious encounter with nature can take place. Through the exercises described in **Dying Forests**, the strength to change one's habits and our destructive technology may emerge. **Dying Forests** is a striking example of the use of Goethe's scientific method which aims to understand the living whole, rather than the dead parts.

Jochen Bockemühl is a scientist working at the Goetheanum Research Laboratory in Dornach, Switzerland. He has lectured and conducted many 'observation workshops' in the English speaking world. His work on plant metamorphosis is included in Open University biology course texts.

Sewn limp bound; full colour cover; 8¼″ × 8¼″ (210 ×210mm); 96pp; 46 water colour illustrations in full colour, plus drawings.
ISBN 1 869 890 02 7

VISION IN ACTION
The art of taking and shaping initiatives.
Christopher Schaefer and Tijno Voors.

Vision is a working book for those involved in taking and shaping initiatives. The authors ask:- How can individuals and groups take initiatives successfully? Once started, how can projects be shaped and developed effectively?

Building on their practical experience of fostering and taking initiatives, the authors offer useful road maps to those developing ventures. Examples are given of community projects, schools, employment initiatives, small businesses, farms, cultural and therapeutic centres.

The road maps include:-
The process of starting and nurturing initiatives;
Ways of working together;
Financing initiatives;

The development phases of initiatives;
Initiatives and individual development.

There are exercises, case studies and questionnaires which can be used by people preparing and reviewing initiatives, or considering their next step.

Christopher Schaefer PhD works in social and community development in the USA. Tÿno Voors works at the centre for Social Development at Emerson College, Sussex.

Sewn limp bound; 8¼″ × 5¼″ (210 × 135mm); 190pp; 3 illustrations.
Not for sale in the USA.
ISBN 0 950 706 29 9

HOPE, EVOLUTION AND CHANGE
John Davy.
Introdution by Owen Barfield.

The twenty-seven articles in this book reflect the author's work as a scientist, journalist and lecturer: articles on evolutionary questions, language, education, science, caring for the planet, life after life, and contemporary thinkers like Schumacher and Elizabeth Kübler-Ross.

Colin Wilson '...a significant figure...' review of **Hope** in **Resurgence**.

Paperback; 8¼″ × 5¼″ (210 × 135mm); 274pp.
ISBN 0 950 706 27 2
To be published in German.

MAN ON THE THRESHOLD
The challenge of inner development.
Bernard Lievegoed, MD.

The author of **Phases** and **Developing Organisations** describes the challenge of inner development today. Eastern and western meditative paths are described, and there are sections on personal development and counselling.

Paperback; full colour cover; 8¼″ × 5¼″ (210 × 135mm); 224pp.
ISBN 0 950 706 26 4

SOCIAL ECOLOGY
Exploring post-industrial society.
Martin Large.

Social Ecology looks at the development of individuals, groups, organisations and society in the post-industrial age.

Paperback; 8¼″ × 5¾″ (210 × 145mm); 162pp.   ISBN 0 950 706 22 1

Social Ecology Series: In Preparation for 1987

RUDOLF STEINER
An introduction.
Rudi Lissau.

This book gives a vivid picture of Rudolf Steiner's life and work. It aims to point out the relevance of Steiner's activities to contemporary social and human concerns. There are chapters on Steiner's philosophy; his view of the universe, earth and the human being; Christ and human destiny; the meditative path; education and social development; approaches to Rudolf Steiner's work and obstacles.

Rudi Lissau has taught adolescents at Wynstones School for over forty years. He has written and lectured widely in North America, the UK, Scandinavia and Central Europe.

Sewn limp bound; 8¼" × 5¼" (210 × 135mm); 192pp approx.
ISBN 1 869 890 06 X

MONEY, SOUL AND SPIRIT
Steve Briault and Glen Saunders.

Money is based on the authors' experience and insights gained through working with money in 'conventional' and 'alternative' settings, including the provision of community banking and advisory services to a wide range of individuals and organisations. Was D. H. Lawrence right when he wrote that money "poisons you when you've got it and starves you when you haven't"? How can we take hold of it in ways which support our bodily existence without enslaving our hearts and minds? How must we change our thinking, feeling and doing so that money can find its healthy place within the human community? The book does not offer tax advice, or tell you how to get rich: it takes its starting point from the fundamental questions people face today with the tremendous broadening of inner and outer choices. New spiritual directions, changing values in relationships, new attitudes to work and to working with others, a stronger sense of individual biography and personal development – all these indicate the context and the need for a change in our perspectives and approaches to money. This will be taken up for organisations, initiative groups and personal life.

Some of the themes covered will be:
managing and metamorphosing money;
possession – needs and wants;
humanising money – overcoming hypnosis and fear;
ensouling investment – savings and lending;
transforming work and payment;
welfare, charity, productivity;
inheritance and dependence.

Stephen Briault works at the Centre for Social Development at Emerson College. Glen Saunders is an accountant and works for Mercury Provident PLC.

Paperback; 8¼" × 5¼" (210 × 136mm); 160pp approx.
ISBN 0 860 890 07 8

DRUGS
The work of ARTA

Drugs (provisional title) addresses the problems of hard drug taking, and the insights gained by the co-workers of ARTA in Holland in assisting drug addicts.

Who's Bringing Them Up? Series

THE CHILDREN'S YEAR
Crafts and clothes for children to make.
Stephanie Cooper, Christine Fynes-Clinton and Marye Rowling.

Here is a book which hopes to give the possibility to adults and children alike to rediscover the joy and satisfaction of making something that they know looks and feels good and which can also be played with imaginatively. It takes us through Spring, Summer, Autumn and Winter with appropriate gifts and toys to create, including full, clear instructions and illustrations. There is children's clothing as well, particularly meant to be made of natural fabrics to let the child's body breathe while growing. There are soft items for play and beauty, and there are firm solid wooden ones; moving toys such as balancing birds or climbing gnomes; horses which move when you add children to them! From woolly hats to play houses, mobiles or dolls, here are 112 potential treasures to make in seasonal groupings.

You needn't be an experienced crafts person to create something lovely, and the illustrations make it a joy to browse through while choosing what to make first. **The Children's Year** offers handwork for all ages and individualities, it reminds us of the process of creating as opposed to merely consuming, and all this in the context of nature's rhythm through the year.

The authors are parents who have tried and tested the things to make included in **The Children's Year**, with their own families.

Paperback or hardback; full colour cover; 10½″ × 8½″ (267mm × 216mm); 220pp; several hundred illustrations.
ISBN 1 869 890 00 0

FESTIVALS, FAMILY AND FOOD
Diana Carey and Judy Large.

'Packed full of ideas on things to do, food to make, songs to sing and games to play, it's an invaluable resources book designed to help you and your family celebrate the various festival days scattered round the year.'

The Observer

Paperback; full colour cover; 10″ × 8″ (250 × 200mm); 216pp; over 200 illustrations.
ISBN 0 950 706 23 X
Fourth impression.

LIFEWAYS
Working with family questions.
Gudrun Davy and Bons Voors.

Lifeways is about children, about family life, about being a parent. But most of all it is about freedom, and how the tension between family life and personal fulfillment can be resolved.

'These essays affirm that creating a family, even if you are a father on your own, or a working mother, can be a joyful, positive and spiritual work. The first essay is one of the wisest and balanced discussions of women's rôles I have read.'

Fiona Handley,
Church of England Newspaper.

Paperback; colour cover; 6″ × 8¼″ (150 × 210mm); 316pp.
ISBN 0 950 706 24 8
Third impression 1985.
Lifeways is published in German and Dutch.

THE INCARNATING CHILD
Joan Salter.

Even in today's modern technological world, the mystery and miracle of conception, pregnancy and birth stir within many people a sense of wonder. **The Incarnating Child** picks up Wordsworth's theme "our Birth is but a sleep and a forgetting . . ." and follows the Soul life of tiny babies well into childhood. It is full of practical advice for mothers, fathers, relations or anyone concerned with childcare. Joan Salter examines pregnancy, birth, early infancy, babyhood, childhood, on up to adolescence. She addresses physical and spiritual development, the formation of healthy personalities, nutrition, clothing, environment, toys and learning, immunization and health, and the acquisition of skills and thinking ability. She writes with an astounding attention to detail, and the voice of years of experience in her field.

Joan Salter is a specialist in maternal and childcare, and has a nursing background which included work with migrants from many countries. She is the founder and director of the Gabriel Baby Centre, since 1976 a centre for maternal and child welfare in Melbourne, and is essentially concerned with the upbringing of the child in the home.

Full colour cover; 8¼″ × 5¼″ (210 × 135mm); 220pp approx.; illustrations and photos.
ISBN 1 869 890 04 3

Orders

If you have difficulties ordering from a bookshop you can order direct from
Hawthorn Press, The Mount, Main Road, Whiteshill, Stroud, Glos. GL6
6JA (Telephone 045 36 - 77040).